# STUDIES IN ZEN

## DAISETZ TEITARO SUZUKI, D. LITT

*Professor of Buddhist Philosophy in the Otani University, Kyoto*

Edited by

## CHRISTMAS HUMPHREYS

*President of the Buddhist Society, London*

A DELTA BOOK

Zen Buddhism

A Delta Book
Published by Dell Publishing Co., Inc.
750 Third Avenue
New York 17, New York
By arrangement with Philosophical Library, Inc.
Published, 1955, by Philosophical Library, Inc.
Library of Congress Catalog Card Number: 55-14253
Manufactured in the United States of America
Second Printing

# CONTENTS

Editor's Foreword      *Page* 8

*Chapter* I   The Zen Sect of Buddhism (1906)    11

II   Zen Buddhism (1938)    48

III   An Interpretation of Zen-Experience (1939)    61

IV   Reason and Intuition in Buddhist Philosophy (1951)    85

V   Zen: A Reply to Dr. Hu Shih (1953)    129

VI   Mondo (1953)    165

VII   The Role of Nature in Zen Buddhism (1953)    176

Index    207

# EDITOR'S FOREWORD

DAISETZ TEITARO SUZUKI, D.Litt., Professor of Buddhist Philosophy in the Otani University, Kyoto, was born in 1869. He is probably now the greatest living authority on Buddhist philosophy, and is certainly the greatest authority on Zen Buddhism. His major works in English on the subject of Buddhism number a dozen or more, and of his works in Japanese as yet unknown to the West there are at least eighteen. He is, moreover, as a chronological bibliography of books on Zen in English clearly shows, the pioneer teacher of the subject outside Japan, for except for Kaiten Nukariya's *Religion of the Samurai* (Luzac & Co. 1913) nothing was known of Zen as a living experience, save to the readers of *The Eastern Buddhist* (1921-1939), until the publication of *Essays in Zen Buddhism* (First Series) in 1927.

Dr. Suzuki writes with authority. Not only has he studied original works in Sanskrit, Pali, Chinese and Japanese, but he has an up-to-date knowledge of Western thought in German and French as well as in the English which he speaks and writes so fluently. He is, moreover, more than a scholar; he is a Buddhist. Though not a priest of any Buddhist sect, he is honoured in every temple in Japan, for his knowledge of spiritual things, as all who have sat at his feet bear witness, is direct and profound. When he speaks of the higher stages of consciousness he speaks as a man who dwells therein, and the impression he makes on those who enter the fringes of his mind is that of a man who seeks for the intellectual symbols wherewith to describe a state of awareness which lies indeed "beyond the intellect".

To those unable to sit at the feet of the Master his writings must be a substitute. All these, however, were out of print in England by 1940, and all remaining stocks in Japan were destroyed in the fire which consumed three-quarters of Tokyo in 1945. When, therefore, I reached Japan in 1946, I arranged with the author for the Buddhist Society, London—my wife and myself as its nominees —to begin the publication of his Collected Works, reprinting the old favourites, and printing as fast as possible translations of the many new works which the Professor, self-immured in his house at Kyoto, had written during the war.

Of Zen itself I need say nothing here, but the increasing sale of books on the subject, such as *The Spirit of Zen* by Alan Watts

(Murray), my own *Zen Buddhism* (Heinemann), and the series of original translations of Chinese Zen Scriptures and other works published by the Buddhist Society, prove that the interest of the West is rising rapidly. Zen, however, is a subject extremely easy to misunderstand, and it is therefore important that the words of a recognized expert should come readily to hand.

The present volume consists of seven articles and lectures which might otherwise be lost to futurity in the archives of the periodicals in which they first appeared. They cover forty-seven years of time (1906-1953), and much of the world in space. They have been selected, revised and arranged in order under the direction of Dr. Suzuki, and the Editor claims no credit for the volume save the suggestion that such magnificent material should be made available to the widest possible public. I am very grateful to the Editors of the periodicals concerned for permission to reprint, and to all those members of the Buddhist Society who have helped in the wearisome task of retyping. The following notes may be of interest to the students of each article.

1. THE ZEN SECT OF BUDDHISM. This is reprinted from *The Journal of the Pali Text Society* for 1906—7. The article was off-printed as a pamphlet, and the copy given by Dr. Suzuki to Alexander Fisher, the distinguished artist who was an early member of the original Buddhist Society of Great Britain and Ireland, at some time fell into the Editor's hands. When he asked Dr. Suzuki's permission to include it in the present volume, the latter asked that the following comment be added:

"This was written in 1906 for the Pali Text Society, and was, I think, the first article I ever wrote on Zen Buddhism. It is based on the traditional history of Zen as transmitted by historians, and does not contain the material later discovered in the Tung-huang MS. The article will, however, give information to students of Zen, especially Western students for whom access to original Chinese sources is difficult. I have made a few necessary corrections in the light of my subsequent studies, but in the main the article stands as originally written."

2. ZEN BUDDHISM. This article is reprinted from *Monumenta Nipponica* for 1938 and is also what Dr. Suzuki calls an early work, written, that is to say, before his views on Zen Buddhism and its development were changed in the light of matured thought and recent discoveries.

3. AN INTERPRETATION OF ZEN EXPERIENCE. This article is taken from *Philosophy—East and West*. edited by Dr. Charles A. Moore and published by the Princetown University Press in 1944, in whom

the copyright is vested. The paper was read to the East—West Philosophers' Conference held in the University of Hawaii during the summer of 1939.

4. REASON AND INTUITION IN BUDDHIST PHILOSOPHY. This paper is taken from *Essays in East—West Philosophy*, edited by Charles A. Moore, and published by the University of Hawaii Press, Honolulu, in 1951. It was read in person by Dr. Suzuki at the second East—West Philosophers' Conference held in Honolulu in the summer of 1949. It is regarded by many as one of the greatest works ever produced by the author.

5. ZEN: A REPLY TO DR. HU SHIH. This is a Reply to an article by Dr. Hu Shih which was printed immediately after the latter's article in the April 1953 issue of *Philosophy East and West*, published by the University of Hawaii Press. For further comment see the Editorial note at the head of the Reply.

6. MONDO. This article was specially written by Dr. Suzuki for the August 1953 issue of *The Middle Way*, the journal of the Buddhist Society, London.

7. THE ROLE OF NATURE IN ZEN BUDDHISM. This was a paper read by Dr. Suzuki at Ascona, Switzerland, in August 1953. It appears in the *Eranos Jahrbuch* published in 1954.

CHRISTMAS HUMPHREYS,
*President of the Buddhist Society, London.*

# I. THE ZEN SECT OF BUDDHISM

## FOREWORD

DURING the twenty centuries of development in the Far
East Buddhism has been differentiated into many sects,
which are so far distinct from their original Hindu types
that we are justified in designating Far-Eastern Buddhism
by a special name. Though, as a matter of course, all these
different sects trace back their final authority to the
Indian founder, and were introduced by Indian mission-
aries into the lands where they have been thriving
throughout their long history, they would not have
reached the present stage of perfection unless they had
been elaborated by Chinese and Japanese geniuses.
Students of Buddhism, therefore, cannot well afford to
ignore or neglect the study of Chinese and Japanese
Buddhism, not only in its historical aspect, but also as a
living and still growing spiritual force.

Among the many sects of Buddhism that developed in
the Far East we find a unique order, which claims to
transmit the essence and spirit of Buddhism directly from
its author, and this not in a form of any written document
or literary legacy. Its scholastic name is the Sect of
Buddha-Heart, but it is popularly known as Zen Sect
(*Dhyana* in Sanskrit, *Jhana* in Pali, *Ch'an* in Chinese).

This sect is unique, not only in Buddhism itself, but, I
believe, also in the history of religion generally. Its
doctrines, broadly speaking, are those of a speculative
mysticism, and they are so peculiarly—sometimes poeti-
cally and sometimes almost enigmatically—represented
and demonstrated, that only those who have actually
gained an insight into them and been trained in the
system can see their ultimate signification. What the Zen
Sect, therefore, most emphatically insists on is one's inner
spiritual enlightenment. It does not find any intrinsic
importance in the sacred *sutras*, or their expositions by

the wise and learned. Subjectivism and individualism are strongly set against traditional authority and objective revelation, and, as the most efficient method of attaining spiritual enlightenment, the followers of the Zen Sect propose the practice of Dhyana (*zenna* in Japanese, and *ch'anna* in Chinese)—that is, contemplation or meditation (1).[1] Hence the name "Zen", which is an abbreviation.

## HISTORY OF THE ZEN SECT

### *India*

According to Zen scholars, their history is considered to have started from the time when Buddha showed a nosegay of some beautiful golden-coloured flowers to a congregation of his disciples on Mount Vulture. The incident is related in a sutra entitled *Dialogue of the Buddha and Mahapitaka Brahmaraja* (2) as follows:

"The Brahmaraja came to a congregation of Buddhists on Mount Vulture, and offering a golden-coloured lotus-flower (*utpala*) to Buddha, prostrated himself on the ground and reverently asked the Master to preach the Dharma for the benefit of sentient beings. Buddha ascended the seat and brought forth the flowers before the congregation of gods and men. But none of them could comprehend the meaning of this act on the part of Buddha, except the venerable Mahakashyapa, who softly smiled and nodded. Then exclaimed Buddha: 'I am the owner of the Eye of the wonderful Dharma, which is Nirvana, the Mind, the mystery of reality and non-reality, and the gate of transcendental truth. I now hand it over to Mahakashyapa.'"

Mahakashyapa transmitted this Eye, which looks into the deeps of the Dharma, to his successor, Ananda, and this transmission is recorded to have taken place in the following manner:

[1] For Notes see pp. 45–7.

Ananda asked Kashyapa: "What was it that thou hast received from Buddha besides the robe and the bowl?" Kashyapa called: "O Ananda." Ananda replied: "Yes." Thereupon Kashyapa said: "Wilt thou take down the flag-pole at the gate?" Upon receiving this order, a spiritual illumination came over the mind of Ananda, and the "Seal of Spirit" was handed over by Mahakashyapa to this junior disciple.

The Zen Sect acknowledges the following twenty-eight patriarchs after Buddha who successfully transmitted the "Seal" down to Bodhidharma, who came to China in the year A.D. 520: (1) Mahakashyapa; (2) Ananda; (3) Sanavasa; (4) Upagupta; (5) Dhrtaka; (6) Micchaka; (7) Vasumitra; (8) Buddhananda; (9) Buddhamitra; (10) Parsva; (11) Punyayasha; (12) Asvaghosha; (13) Kapimala; (14) Nagarjuna; (15) Kanadeva; (16) Rahurata; (17) Sanghananda; (18) Kayasata; (19) Kumarata; (20) Jnayata; (21) Vasubandhu; (22) Manura; (23) Haklena; (24) Simha; (25) Bhagasita; (26) Punyamitra; (27) Prajnatara; (28) Bodhidharma (usually abbreviated Dharma). (3)

### China

Bodhidharma, the twenty-eighth patriarch in India and the first in China, was the third son of the King of Hsiang-chih (Kasi?) in Southern India. He became a monk after he had reached manhood, and studied Buddhism under Prajnatara for some forty years, it is said. After the death of his teacher, he assumed the patriarchal authority of the Dhyana school, and energetically fought for sixty years or more against heterodox schools. After this, in obedience to the instruction which he had received from Prajnatara, he sailed for China, spending three years on the way. In the year 520 he at last landed at Kuang-chou in Southern China. The Emperor Wu, of the Liang dynasty, at once invited him to proceed to his capital, Chin-liang (modern Nanking). The Emperor was a most devoted Buddhist, and did everything to promote the interests of his religion, but this not without a personal consideration. Therefore, as soon as his reverend guest from the West was settled in his palace, his first question was: "I have built so many temples and monasteries, I have copied so many sacred books of Buddha, I have converted so many Bhikshus and Bhikshunis; now what merit does your reverence think I have thus accumulated?" To this, however, the founder of the Zen Sect in China coldly and curtly replied: "Your Majesty, no merit whatever."

The Emperor Wu asked him again: "What is considered by your reverence to be the first principle of the Holy Doctrine?" Said Dharma: "Vast emptiness, and nothing holy therein." The Emperor could not comprehend the signification of this answer, and made another query: "Who is he, then, that now confronts me?"

By this he perhaps meant that, if there were nothing but vast emptiness and absolute transcendentality in the first principle of existence, why, then, do we have here a world of contrasts and relations? Are not some of us regarded as holy and others wicked? And Bodhidharma, who stands at this moment before the Emperor, belongs to the first class. How is it that his answer seems to contradict the facts of experience? Hence the question: "Who is he, then, that now confronts me?" It is interesting to notice the similarity between this conversation and the first talk between the Greek King Milinda and Nagasena (Rhys Davids, *Questions of King Milinda*, Vol. I, pp. 40-45).

But Dharma was the apostle of mysticism, and scholastic discussion did not appeal to him. His reply was quite terse: "I know not, Your Majesty!"

Being convinced that his august patron was not qualified to embrace his faith, Dharma left the State of Liang and went to the State of Northern Wei, where he retired into the Shao-lin monastery. It is said that he spent all his time, during a period of nine years there, silently sitting against the wall and deeply absorbed in meditation, and for this singular habit he is said to have earned the title of "the wall-gazing brahmin".

Finally, there came to him a former Confucian scholar, named Shen Kuang, who, not being satisfied with the teaching of his native teacher, decided to follow the faith of Dharma. The latter, however, seemed to have altogether ignored this man, for he did not pay any attention to the earnest supplication of this seeker of truth. We are told that Shen Kuang in the face of this cold reception stood in the snow on the same spot throughout seven days and nights. At last he cut off one of his arms with the sword he was carrying in his girdle, and presenting this before the imperturbable Dharma, he said: "This is a token of my sincere desire to be instructed in your faith. I have been seeking peace of mind these many years, but to no purpose. Pray, your reverence, have my soul (*hsin*) pacified."

Dharma then answered: "Where is your soul? Bring it out before me, and I shall have it pacified." Shen Kuang said: "The very reason of my trouble is that I am unable to find the soul." Whereupon Dharma exclaimed: "There! I have pacified your soul." And Shen Kuang all at once attained spiritual enlightenment, which removed all his doubts and put an end to all his struggles.

Dharma died in the year 528, at the age, according to tradition, of about 150. Shen Kuang (485–593) was given by Bodhidharma the Buddhist name Hui-kʻo, and became the second patriarch of the Zen Sect in China.

Hui-kʻo handed over the "Seal of Buddha-Heart" to his foremost disciple, Seng-Tsʻan (died 606), who was successively followed by Tao-hsin (died 651) and Hung-jen (died 675). After Hung-jen the Sect was divided into two schools, Southern and Northern. The latter, representing heterodoxy, had no issue, and made no further development; but the Southern school, which was led by Hui-neng, the sixth patriarch, continued the orthodox line of transmission, which, though long inactive and almost dead in its land of birth, is still flourishing in Japan. (4)

The sixth patriarch, Hui-neng, was a great religious

genius, and his life marks an epoch in the history of the Zen Sect in the Far East. It was due to him that his Sect, hitherto comparatively inactive and rather tending to ascetic quietism, now assumed a more energetic role in the demonstration of its peculiar features, and began to make its influence more and more felt, especially among the thoughtful class of people.

His missionary activities began immediately after the death of his predecessor, Hung-jen—that is, in the year 675. He gathered about himself many able disciples, through whom the Sect made rapid development, dividing itself into several schools. Of these two, Rinzai (Lin-chi) and Soto (Ts'ao-tung), enjoyed prosperity throughout the T'ang (618–905) and the Sung (960–1278) dynasties, which were the golden age of the Zen Sect. A collection of the sermons of the sixth patriarch, known as *Fa pao t'an ching*, was incorporated in the Chinese collection of the Buddhist sacred books, and is considered one of the most authoritative works of the Zen Sect. (We shall give quotations from this book later on.)

An interesting story is told of the sixth patriarch, Hui-neng—how he came to succeed Hung-jen in his religious authority. The fifth patriarch wished to select his spiritual heir among his many disciples, and one day made the announcement that anyone who could prove his thorough comprehension of the religion would be given the patriarchal robe, and proclaimed as his legitimate successor. According to this, one of his disciples, who was very learned and thoroughly versed in the lore of his religion, and who was therefore considered by his brethren in faith to be in possession of an unqualified right to the honour, composed a stanza expressing his view, and posted it on the outside wall of the meditation hall, which read:

> This body is the Bodhi-tree;
> The soul is like a mirror bright:
> Take heed to keep it always clean,
> And let not dust collect on it.

All those who read these lines were greatly impressed, and secretly cherished the idea that the author of the gatha would surely be awarded the prize. But when they awoke next morning, they were surprised to see another written alongside of it, which ran as follows:

The Bodhi is not like the tree;
The mirror bright is nowhere shining:
As there is nothing from the first,
Where can the dust itself collect?

The writer of these lines was an insignificant lay-brother, who spent most of his time in pounding rice for the brotherhood. He had such an unassuming air that nobody ever thought much of him, and therefore the entire monastery was now set astir to see this bold challenge made upon its recognized authority. But the fifth patriarch saw in this unpretentious lay-brother a future leader of mankind, and decided to transfer to him the mantle of his office. He had, however, some misgivings concerning the matter, for the majority of his disciples were not enlightened enough to see anything of deep religious intuition in the lines composed by the rice-pounder, Hui-neng; and if he were awarded the prize they might do him violence. So the fifth patriarch gave a secret sign to Hui-neng to come to his room at midnight, when the rest of the brotherhood was fast asleep. Then he gave him the bowl and robe as insignia of his patriarchal authority in appreciation of his unsurpassable spiritual attainment, and with the assurance that the future of their faith would be brighter than ever. The patriarch then advised him that it would be wise for him to hide his own light under a bushel, until the proper time arrived for his public appearance and active propaganda.

Before the day broke, however, the news of what had happened in secret became noised abroad throughout the monastery, and a party of indignant monks, headed by one named Ming, pursued the fugitive, Hui-neng, who, in accordance with his master's instruction, was secretly leaving the monastery. When he was overtaken by the pursuers while crossing a mountain-pass not far away, he laid down his robe and bowl on a rock nearby, and said to the monk Ming: "This robe symbolizes our patriarchal faith and is not to be carried away by force. Take it along with thee, however, if thou so desirest."

Ming tried to lift it, but it was as heavy as a mountain. He halted, hesitated, and trembled with awe. At last he said: "I come here to obtain the faith and not the robe. O my brother monk, pray dispel my ignorance."

Said the sixth patriarch: "If thou comest for the faith, stop all thy hankerings. Thinkest thou not of good, thinkest thou not of evil, and see what at this moment thy own face doth look like, which thou hadst even prior to thy birth?"

Being thus questioned, Ming at once perceived the fundamental reason of things, which he had hitherto sought in things without. He now understood everything, as if he had taken a cupful of cold water and tasted it to his own satisfaction. Out of the immensity of his feeling he was literally bathed in tears and perspiration, and most reverently approaching the patriarch he saluted him, and asked: "Beside this hidden sense as embodied in those significant words, is there any other thing which is secret?"

The patriarch answered: "In what I have shown to thee there is nothing hidden. If thou reflectest within thyself and recognizest thine own face, which was before the world, secrecy is in thyself."

Under Hui-neng, who died 713, the Sect was divided into two schools, represented by two of his foremost disciples, Nangaku (Nan-yüeh) and Seigen (Ch'ing-yüan). Hui-neng was the last in the patriarchal line of the Zen Sect. He did not hand down his official insignia to his successors, for he feared that it might cause unnecessary strife and undesirable schism, as illustrated in his own case. With him, therefore, the history of the

Zen Sect must be said to turn over a new leaf, not only externally but inwardly. The patriarchal system was destroyed, the question of heterodoxy and orthodoxy was no more; and any leader who was duly trained under a recognized master, and received his sanction for his spiritual attainment, was at liberty to develop the faith and practice of the Zen Sect in any manner best suited to his individuality. Nan-yüeh (died 744) and Ch'ing-yüan (died 740) equally represented the orthodox line of their common faith, the difference between the two schools being that one emphasized one aspect and the other another.

From the time of Nan-yüeh and Ch'ing-yüan onwards the Zen Sect made steady progress and gained greater influence among all classes of people, but especially among the educated. During the T'ang dynasty, under which Chinese culture and civilization may be said to have reached its consummation, was the time when Buddhism became thoroughly naturalized in China. It discarded its Hindu garb, borrowed and ill-fitting, and began to weave its own, entirely with native materials and in accord with Chinese taste. Though the doctrinal phase of Buddhism was not yet quite assimilated by the Chinese mind, the Zen Sect developed along its own peculiar line, and became thoroughly Chinese. (This will be more clearly recognized when we treat later of the faith and practice of the Zen Sect.) The greatest masters of Zen were almost all the product of this age, covering a space of about 800 years—that is, roughly, from the middle of the T'ang dynasty to the end of the Sung. Many eminent scholars, poets, statesmen, and artists rapped at the monastery door, and greatly enjoyed conversation with the Zen masters. Influence on Chinese culture given by those lay disciples of the Sect was considerable. Almost all the important temples and monasteries now existing in the Middle Kingdom belong to the Zen Sect, though the Sect as a living faith is as good as dead. And from this it can be inferred how great must have been the influence the Zen Sect exercised when at the zenith of its prosperity in the latter part of the T'ang and throughout the Sung dynasty.

## Japan

In Japan at present we have two schools of the Zen Sect, Soto (Ts'ao-tung) and Rinzai (Lin-chi). The former traces back its long ancestral line to the Ch'ing-yüan school, and the latter originated with Rinzai (died 867), who flourished during the middle period of the T'ang dynasty and succeeded the line represented by Nan-yüeh under the sixth patriarch. The Soto school was introduced into Japan by Dogen, A.D. 1233, who went over to China early in the thirteenth century, and was duly authorized by his master Tendo Nyojo (T'ien-T'ung Ju-Ching, died 1228), of the Ch'ing-yüan line. The Rinzai school was officially established in the year 1191 by Yesai. The Hojo family, which was the real head of the Government at that time, greatly encouraged the dissemination of Zen teaching. This resulted in frequent communication between the Chinese and the Japanese masters. And a large number of capable leaders who arose one after another kept up the vitality of Zen faith throughout the succeeding three or four hundred years.

At present the two schools of the Zen Sect in Japan are sharing the common fate of Buddhism in the twentieth century—that is, they are in a stage of transition from a medieval, dogmatic, and conservative spirit to one of progress, enlightenment, and liberalism. The Rinzai school is more speculative and intellectual, while the Soto tends towards quietism. The latter is numerically strong and the former qualitatively so. The recent war[1] in the Far East has served to reawaken the old spirit of nationalism, and young Japan is anxiously investigating its moral and spiritual legacy, the wealth and significance of which it has only recently begun to appreciate.

[1] The Russo-Japanese War.

## PRINCIPLES OF THE ZEN SECT

### *Facts and not words*

The Zen Sect is what Western scholars might call mysticism, though its characteristic development and its practical method of discipline are as different from Christian mysticism as Buddhism generally is from Christianity. The latter has always endeavoured to acknowledge the objective existence of a supreme being, or the transcendentality of a universal reason. The German school of mysticism, indeed, almost converted Christianity into pantheism and tried to find God within one's own being. But there is no denying the fact that the Christian mystics were deviating from the original path of Jewish monotheism, which is really the most prominent feature of Christianity. Buddhism, on the other hand, has shown what some people consider a pantheistic tendency from the beginning of its history, and though at a certain stage of its development it was disposed towards ethical positivism, it has always encouraged the practice of Dhyana as a means of enlightenment. It is no wonder that this special discipline came to be emphasized above all others as a saving power, when the Buddhist faith began to wither under the baneful influence of scholasticism. Though mysticism has been frequently misinterpreted and condemned, there is no doubt that it is the soul of the religious life, that it is what gives to a faith its vitality, fascination, sublimity and stability. Without mysticism the religious life has nothing to be distinguished from the moral life, and, therefore, whenever a faith becomes conventionalized, and devoid, for some reason or other, of its original enthusiasm, mysticism invariably comes to its rescue. The recrudescence of Buddhist mysticism in India, and its introduction into China and Japan, is also due to this law of the human mind.

Quite in accordance with this view, the Zen Sect

teaches us to disregard or discard the entire treasure of Buddhist lore as something superfluous, for it is no more than a second-hand commentary on the mind, which is the source of enlightenment and the proper subject of study. Zen labels itself as "a special transmission outside the canonical teaching of Buddha", and its practical method of salvation is "directly to grasp the Mind and attain Buddhahood". It does not rely upon the sutras or abhidharmas, however exalted and enlightened be the authors of these sacred books. For the ultimate authority of Zen faith is within one's self and not without. A finger may be needed to point at the moon, but ignorant must they be who take the pointer for the real object and altogether forget the final aim of the religious life. The sacred books are useful as far as they indicate the direction where our spiritual efforts are to be applied, and their utility goes no further. Zen, therefore, proposes to deal with concrete living facts, and not with dead letters and theories.

## No Sutras, No Books

The Zen Sect thus has no particular canonical books considered as the final authority for its teachings, nor has it any ready-made set of tenets which have to be embraced by its followers as essential to their spiritual welfare. What it claims to have transmitted from Buddha is his spirit—that is, his enlightened subjectivity, through which he was able to produce so many sacred books. It was this same spirit of the founder of Buddhism that Dharma wanted to instil into the people of the Middle Kingdom.

When Dharma thought, according to the *Transmission of the Lamp* (Fas. III), that the time had come for him to return to his native land he told his disciples: "The time is coming, and why do you not tell me what each one of you has attained?"

Dofuku (Tao-fu), one of the disciples, said: "According to my insight, the Tao operates neither depending upon letters nor separate from them." Dharma said: "You have my skin."

Soji (Tsung-ch'ih), the nun, said: "According to my understanding, it is like Ananda's seeing the land of Akshobhya-Buddha: it is seen once and never seen twice." Dharma said: "You have my flesh."

Doiku (Tao-yu) said: "The four elements are from the first empty and the five aggregates (skandhas) are non-existent. According to my view there is not one object which is said to be attainable." Dharma said: "You have my bones."

Finally Yeka (Hui-k'o) came out, made his bow and took his place. Dharma then said: "You have my marrow."

In such wise the Zen masters handled their religion. They were boldly original and not at all hampered by any traditional teaching of Buddha. Indeed, Buddha himself had frequently to suffer a rather unkind treatment at the hands of his Zen followers. Rinzai, for instance, the founder of the Rinzai school, once made this declaration:

"O you, followers of the Way, do not consider Buddha a consummation of being. As I see him he is like unto a cesspool. Bodhisattvas and Arhats—they are all instruments that will fetter you like the cangue and chain. Therefore, Manjusri kills Gautama with his sword while Anglimala wounds the Shakya with his knife. O you, followers of the Way, there is no Buddhahood that is attainable. Such teachings as 'the triple vehicle', 'the five classes of beings', 'the perfect doctrine', 'the abrupt doctrine', and so on—they are all so many means employed for the curing of various diseases; they are not realities at all. Whatever reality they may claim, they are no more than symbolic representations, they do not go any further than an idle disposition of letters. So I declare.

"O you, followers of the Way, there are some bald-headed fellows who try to find something on which they can work and which would release them thus from worldly bondage. They are altogether mistaken. When a man seeks a Buddha he misses him; when he seeks the Way he misses it; when he seeks a patriarch he misses him."

It is apparent, then, that Zen teachers endeavoured in their missionary work to make their disciples as original and independent as possible, not only in their interpretation of traditional Buddhism but in regard to their ways of thinking. If there was one thing with which they were intensely disgusted, it was blind acceptance of an outside authority and a meek submission to conventionality. They wanted life and individuality and inspiration. They gave perfect freedom to the self-unfolding of the Mind within one's self, which was not to be obstructed by any artificial instruments of torture, such as worshipping the Buddha as a saviour, a blind belief in the sacred books, or an unconditioned reliance upon an outside authority. They advised their followers not to accept anything until it was proved by themselves to be true. Everything, holy or profane, had to be rejected as not belonging to one's inner Mind. Do not cling to the senses, they said; do not cling to intellection; do not rely upon dualism, nor upon monism; do not be carried away by an absolute nor by a God; but be yourself even as you are, and you will be as vast as space, as free as the bird in the air or the fish in water, and your spirit will be as transparent as the mirror. Buddha or no-Buddha, God or no-God, all this is quibbling, a mere playing on words, without real significance.

## Ko-An

The Dhyana masters thus naturally had no stereotyped method of instructing their disciples, nor had the latter any regular routine work to go through. The teachers gave instructions offhand whenever and wherever they pleased, and the pupils came to them when they had something to ask them. In the monastery each of them had his own share of work, for the buildings, grounds,

farm, kitchen, daily religious services, and other miscel-
laneous affairs had to be attended to by the monks. If
they had nothing special to come to the teacher for and
were satisfied with their lot as monks, they stayed there,
quietly observing all the rules relative to the monkish life.
They seem to have all acted upon their own initiative in
the study of Zen.

The following incident in the life of Rinzai, who lived
in the first half of the ninth century, well illustrates the
monastery life which was prevalent in China then and
later.

When Rinzai was assiduously applying himself to Zen
discipline under Obaku (Huang-po, died 850), the head
monk recognized his genius. One day the elder monk
asked him how long he had been in the monastery, to
which Rinzai replied: "Three years." The elder said:
"Have you ever approached the master and asked his
instruction in Buddhism?" Rinzai said: "I have never
done this, for I did not know what to ask." "Why, you
might go to the master and ask him: 'What is the
essence of Buddhism?' " This was the elder's advice.

Rinzai, according to his advice, approached Obaku
and repeated the question, and before he finished the
master gave him blows with his staff.

When Rinzai came back, the elder asked how the
interview went. Said Rinzai: "Before I could finish my
questioning, the master gave me blows of the staff, but I
fail to grasp its meaning." The elder said: "You go to
him again and ask the same question." When he did so,
he received the same response from the master. But
Rinzai was urged again to try it for the third time, yet
the outcome did not improve.

He at last went to the elder and said: "In obedience to
your kind suggestion, I have repeated my question three
times, and been slapped three times. I deeply regret that,
owing to my stupidity, I am unable to comprehend the
hidden meaning of all this. I shall leave this place and go
somewhere else." Said the elder: "If you wish to depart,
do not fail to go and see the master to bid him farewell."

Immediately after this, the elder saw the master, and said: "That young novice who asked you about Buddhism three times is a remarkable fellow. When he comes to take leave of you, be so gracious as to direct him properly. After a hard training he will prove to be a great master, and, like a huge tree, he will give a refreshing shelter to the world."

When Rinzai came to see the master, the latter advised him not to go anywhere else but to Daigu (Tai-yu), of Kao-an, for he would be able to instruct him in the faith.

Rinzai went to Daigu, who asked him whence he came. Being informed that he was from Obaku, Daigu further inquired what instruction he had under the master. Rinzai answered: "I asked him three times about the essence of Buddhism, and he struck me three times. But I am yet unable to see whether I had any fault or not." Daigu said: "Obaku was tender-hearted even as a dotard, and you are not warranted at all to come over here and ask me whether anything was faulty with you."

Being thus reprimanded, the significance of the whole affair suddenly dawned upon the mind of Rinzai, and he exclaimed: "There is not much, after all, in the Buddhism of Obaku." Whereupon Daigu took hold of him, and said: "This ghostly good-for-nothing creature! A few minutes ago you came to me and complainingly asked what was wrong with you, and now you boldly declare that there is not much in the Buddhism of Obaku. What is the reason of all this? Speak! speak!" In response to this, Rinzai softly struck three times with his fist at the ribs of Daigu. The latter then released him, saying: "Your teacher is Obaku, and I have nothing to do with you."

Rinzai took leave of Daigu and came back to Obaku, who, on seeing him come, exclaimed: "Foolish fellow! What does it avail you to come and go all the time like this?" Rinzai said: "It is all due to your doting kindness."

When, after the usual salutation, Rinzai stood by the side of Obaku, the latter asked him whence he had come this time. Rinzai answered: "In obedience to your kind instruction, I was with Daigu. Thence am I come." And he related, being asked for further information, all that had happened there.

Obaku said: "As soon as that fellow [i.e. Daigu] shows himself up here, I shall have to give him a good thrashing."

"You need not wait for him to come; have it right this moment," was the reply; and with this Rinzai gave his master a slap on the shoulder.

Obaku said: "How dare this lunatic come into my presence and play with the tiger's whiskers!"

Rinzai then burst out into a *"Ho"* (5) and Obaku said: "Attendant, come and carry this lunatic away to his cell." (6)

All such incidents as these soon became known throughout the country, for the monks were constantly travelling from one monastery to another, and the incidents, that is, encounters with the masters, were made subjects of discussion among the monks. Later they came to be technically known as *ko-an* (*kung-an* in Chinese), literally meaning "official record", or a "judicial case" to be examined before a tribunal of the Zen jurists. During the Sung dynasty, about the time of Aoso Hoyen (Wutsu Fayen, died 1104), these records were used by the master for training his pupils, as the means of making them attain spiritual enlightenment. A few instances are given here:

1. A monk asked Tozan (Tung-shan, 806–869): "Who is Buddha?" And the master replied: "Three pounds of flax." (7)

2. A monk asked Suibi (T'sui-wei): "What is the significance of the first patriarch's coming over to China?" (This is considered to be tantamount to asking the first principle of Buddhism.) Suibi said: "Wait till nobody is around here, and I shall tell you of it." They entered into the garden, when the monk said: "There is nobody about here. I pray you tell me." Suibi then pointed at the bamboos, saying: "This bamboo has grown so high, and that one is rather short." (8)

3. Rinzai once delivered a sermon before a gathering

of his disciples, in which he said: "Upon this mass of red-coloured flesh there abideth an untitled true man. He constantly cometh out and in from your sense-gates (9). Those who have not yet testified this, behold, behold." A monk came out of the rank, and asked: "Who is this untitled true man?" The master descended from the chair and took hold of this monk, saying: "Speak, speak!" The monk faltered, whereupon, releasing him, Rinzai remarked: "What a worthless stuff is this untitled true man!" Without a further remark he returned to his room.

As is seen in these "judicial cases", what Zen masters aim to attain is not a secret communion with a Supreme Being, or a hypnotic absorption in the absolute, or the dreaming of a divine vision, or forgetting one's self in a vast emptiness where all marks of particularity vanish leaving only the blankness of the unconscious. Their efforts are directed to bring us in contact with Being or Life which animates all things, and personally feel its pulsation, as when the eye comes in touch with light it recognizes it as light. When one has this actual inner feeling, which might be called intuition or immediate knowledge, as Western philosophers have it, Zen teachers designate such a one a Buddha, or Bodhisattva, or a Daizen Chishiki (great, good, wise man).

## NOT ASCETICISM

Those who are only acquainted with the ascetic phase or the pessimistic phase of Buddhism may think that the Zen Sect shares it too; but the fact is that the Zen is one of the most positive and energetic sects of Buddhism. Be only in accord, it teaches, with the reason of the universe, and the enlightened do not see anything in the world of the senses to be condemned or shunned, as is done by ascetics or pessimists. In this respect the members of the Zen Sect are like other Mahayanists—that is, they regard sympathy and loving-kindness as the very foundation of their religion. For they refuse to remain in their exalted spiritual position and to leave all their fellow-creatures suffering in ignorance. They come down into this world of particulars, as it were, from their idealistic altitude. They live like the masses; they suffer, endure, and hope. But their inner life is not disturbed by any tribulation of this world. The process of spiritual development of a Zen follower is pictorially illustrated in the popular book called *Ju Gyu no Zu*—that is, *The Ten Ox-herding Pictures*—in which the spiritual training of the Zen Sect is likened to the taming of an ox.

## PHILOSOPHY OF ZEN

No attempt will here be made to expound the philosophy of Zen which underlies those enigmatic *ko-an*, a few samples of which have been given above, but I shall limit myself to giving to the reader a translation of certain passages in the "Sermons of the Sixth Patriarch" (*Fa pao t'an ching*), which was really an epoch-making work in the history of the Zen Sect. The book was compiled by his disciples from their notebooks. (10)

"Have your hearts thoroughly purified, and think of the Maha-prajna-paramita. O my good and intelligent brethren, all beings are from the beginning in possession of the Bodhi-prajna [transcendental intelligence or wisdom], and the reason why they are unable to realize it is due to their confused subjectivity. You should, therefore, exert yourselves according to the instruction of a great enlightened teacher, and have an insight into the nature of being. The Buddha-nature is the same in the ignorant as in the intelligent; but as there is a difference between enlightenment and confusion, some are called benighted, while others are enlightened. I shall now speak about the doctrine of Maha-prajna-paramita, and lead you to the way of intelligence. Listen to me with hearts true and sincere, as I speak unto you.

"O my good and intelligent brethren, people are talking all the time about Prajna, but they do not compre-

hend the Prajna of their own being. It is like talking about
food, which does not satisfy the appetite. If they keep on
only talking about the supraphenomenal, there will never
be a time when they actually have an insight into it. Mere
talking is of no avail.

"O my good and intelligent brethren, Maha-prajna-
paramita is a Sanskrit term and means in our language
'the great intelligence that leads to the other shore'. This
should be practised in your own heart, and not be talked
about with your lips. If talked about and not practised, it
is like unto a mirage, phantom, dew, or lightning. If
talked about as well as practised, the heart and the mouth
are in harmony.

"The Buddha is the Essence of your being; outside of
it there is no Buddha.

"What is *maha*? *Maha* means 'great'. The vastness of
the mind is like space: it has no limits, it is neither
square nor circular, it is neither large nor small. It has no
colour, such as blue, yellow, red, or white. It has also no
magnitude, such as high or low, long or short. It is,
again, free from anger and joy; it is above yes and no,
good and evil. It has no tail or head.

"The land of all the Buddhas is like the vastness of
space. The very Essence of our being is from the first
devoid of determinations, and there is nothing particular
which could be taken hold of like an object of sense. When
I speak of the absolute emptiness of our Essence, it should
be understood in this sense. O my good and intelligent
brethren, take heed, however, not to cling to emptiness
when I speak thus. This is most important—not to cling
to emptiness  [or no-determinates]. For those who sit
quietly absorbed in the contemplation of the absolute
[that is, the empty] are sinking in blank nothingness.

"O my good and intelligent brethren, space, as we
see it about us, embraces all material forms, such as the
sun, moon, stars, and constellations, mountains, rivers,
and the great earth, the bubbling springs and the murmuring rivulets, grasses, trees, woods and thickets, good
men as well as bad, heaven as well as hell, and all the

great oceans and all the mountains of Sumeru. Do they not all exist in space? When I speak of the emptiness of Self-essence, it should be understood in the same way.

"O my good and intelligent brethren, the Self-essence embraces all things, and on that account it is called 'great'. All things exist in the Essence of every sentient being. When you see good and evil existing in this world, do not cling to them, nor shun them, nor be defiled by them. The Mind is like unto space, and it is called great—that is, *maha*.

"O my good and intelligent brethren, they that are confused talk with the mouth, while the wise practise in the heart. Again, they that are confused sometimes sit quietly and disturbed by no thoughts, and they think they are great. Such people as these are not worth mentioning, for their views are faulty.

"O my good and intelligent brethren, the capacity of the Mind is great, and there is not a spot in this universe where it does not prevail. When it is working it is manifest, and through this apparent working we come to the knowledge of all things. All is one and one is all. Coming or going, it knows no restraint; the Mind is in its essence freedom, it is Prajna. O my good and intelligent brethren, all Prajna-wisdom grows out of your Self-essence, and does not come from without. Take heed to avoid errors, for this is the free operation of your inner Reason. Be true to yourselves, and everything else will come out true. The Mind's capacity is great and its working universal; it is not concerned with details. Do not commit yourselves to mere talking all day. If you do not practise this in your hearts, you are like unto a man of low birth calling himself a king, which is unrealizable in him. Such persons cannot be called my disciples.

"O my good and intelligent brethren, what is Prajna? Prajna means in our language 'intelligence'. If in all places and at all times your every thought is not benighted, and you always put your intelligence into work, this is Prajnacara. When even a single thought of yours is benighted, Prajna is lost; when even a single thought of yours is enlightened, Prajna is manifest there. People are so benighted and confused that they do not perceive Prajna and yet speak of it. Even when the Mind is not clear, they pretend to be perceiving Prajna. They talk all the time about emptiness, and know not what real emptiness means, for Prajna has no particular form, being the Mind itself. One who understands in this wise knows what Prajna-intelligence is.

"What is *paramita*? It is the Western language, and means in this land 'to reach the other shore'—that is to say, to be free from births and deaths. When you are fettered by the phenomenal, there is birth-and-death, as the waves are stirred in water, and that we call 'this shore'. When you are not attached to the phenomenal, there is no birth-and-death, as water eternally flowing, and that we call 'the other shore' or *paramita*.

"O my good and intelligent brethren, confused are they that do mere talking, for at the moment of their thinking they have committed blunders and wrongs. To practise Prajna in every thought, this is in accord with your inner Reason. Those who are enlightened in this matter understand Prajnadharma, and those who discipline themselves in this principle are practising Prajnacara. They are common mortals who do not discipline themselves in this, while they are Buddhas who practise this in their thought.

"O my good and intelligent brethren, common mortals are Buddhas, and all the passions and desires are born of Wisdom [or Enlightenment, *bodhi*]. As long as your thoughts are confused you are common mortals, but at the very moment you are enlightened you are Buddhas. When your Mind is fettered by sensuality, every desire you cherish is defiled; but as soon as your Mind is freed from the bondage, every desire of yours is born of Wisdom. O good and intelligent brethren, the Maha-prajna-paramita is to be most honoured, has no equal, and stands all alone. It does not depart, nor does it come, and all the Buddhas of the past, present, and future are born of it. By the operation of this great Prajna all the passions, desires, and sensualities are destroyed that arise from the five Skandhas. By thus disciplining one's self, Buddhahood is attained, and the three venomous passions are converted into morality, tranquillity, and wisdom.

"O my good and intelligent brethren, from this spiritual gate of one Prajna there have issued 84,000 forms of wisdom. Why? Because 84,000 different forms of evil passions are possessed by sentient beings. If they were free from sensuality, wisdom which is never independent of one's inner Reason would be manifest all the time. They that are enlightened have no hankering, no repentance, no attachment. In them there is no hypocrisy awakened. Through the operation of one's own true inner Reason, which is no more than Prajna itself, reflect upon all things and illuminate them, and cling not to them nor shun them. This is the way in which the Reason is perceived and Buddhahood is attained."

## Zen and General Culture

### China

Apart from the general influence of Buddhism upon Chinese thought, Zen discipline seems to have been singularly acceptable to the Oriental people. Through the medium of the Zen Sect, Indian Buddhism can be said to have been thoroughly naturalized in the Middle Kingdom and also in Japan. It is not so elaborately speculative as some other Buddhist sects, such as the T'ien T'ai, the Avatamsaka, the Madhyamika, or the Yoga, and this simplicity particularly suited the practical tendency of the Chinese mind. The Zen does not antagonize the doctrines of Confucius, as does Taoism, but instead absorbs them within itself as a part of its practical discipline, and this must have been very gratifying to the Confucians, who are fond of rituals and advocate formalism. Again, the Zen has something in it which savours of Taoism, as it teaches non-attachment to things worldly and a mystic appreciation of Nature, and this must have satisfied the Laotzean elements of the country. In short, the Zen is so elastic, so comprehensive, and so ready to reconcile itself to its environment that it finally came to contain within itself everything that was needed by the Chinese mind. No wonder, then, that its influence among the educated as well as the masses was almost phenomenal since its definite establishment in the middle part of the T'ang dynasty. If in those days the Zen Sect had not existed, the repeated persecutions might have entirely wiped out all traces of Buddhist influence in China, and the re-suscitation of Chinese speculative philosophy in the Sung dynasty (960–1278) and the Ming (1368–1628) might have been an impossibility.

Zen teachers in China used most popular and most forcible language instead of foreign, borrowed Sanskrit-Chinese, and this fact must be considered to have not a little contributed to its universal propagation. Almost all the noted monasteries in China at present belong to the Zen Sect, though the monks no more manifest the spirit of the ancient masters. A great majority of those Confucian scholars or cultured officials who are at all acquainted with Buddhism have gained their knowledge from Zen literature. From towards the end of the T'ang dynasty scholars and statesmen who were worthy of note came to the Zen monasteries, and either submitted themselves to the discipline or delved deeply into its mysterious literature. The tradition seems to be still alive among the educated Chinese of the present day. And the strange fact is that, in spite of their denunciation of the literary demon-stration of the faith, the Zen teachers have produced many writings with a style peculiarly their own.

## Japan

The Zen Sect was introduced into Japan in its per-fected form at the time when feudalism began to take hold of the country—that is, in the Kamakura period. Its sim-

plicity, directness, and efficiency instantly won the heart
of the warrior, and the samurais began to knock at the
monastery gate. The Zen does not share those peculiarities
of early Buddhism which were acceptable only to people
of the leisure classes, nor has it anything to do with
pessimism, passivity, or non-resistance. The military class
of Japan, which had for long been seeking a religion to
satisfy their spiritual needs, at once found their ideal in
the teachings of Zen. The so-called Hojo period in the
history of Japan, which is noted for able administration,
simplicity of life, and the efficiency and energy of the
military class, had thus successfully started the Zen Sect
in the land of the Rising Sun. The Zen monasteries still
extant in Kamakura, the ancient capital of the Hojo
Government, are monuments of the devotion of its
adherents.

The Ashikaga Shogunate that succeeded the Hojo, as
well as the Imperial House of those days, greatly pat-
ronized Zen, which now thoroughly permeates every fibre
of Japanese life and civilization. Not only emperors,
statesmen, and generals came to see Zen masters, but also
men of letters, artists, singers, actors, wrestlers, mer-
chants, masters of tea ceremony, and swordsmen.
They could not withstand the overwhelming tide of the
mystic discipline which is considered to hold the key to
the secrets of life and the universe.

Bushido, the Way of the Samurai, which has come
lately to be much talked of since the conclusion of the
Russo-Japanese War, owes its development to a considerable extent to the Zen Sect. It is, in fact, a production of
the three moral forces in Japan—Shintoism, Confucianism, and Buddhism. Each of them has contributed something to the formation of this code of the knighthood of
Japan. According to the positions taken by different
critics, the share of each of these contributing elements
may be emphasized or underrated; but no fair observer
will deny that Zen had a great deal to do with the religious
and spiritual aspect of Bushido. For the *Lebensanschauung*
of Bushido is no more nor less than that of Zen. The calm-

ness and even joyfulness of heart at the moment of death which is conspicuously observable among the Japanese, the intrepidity which is generally shown by the Japanese soldiers in the face of an overwhelming enemy, and the fairplay shown to the opponent, so strongly taught by Bushido—all these come from the spirit of the Zen training, and not from any such blind, fatalistic conception as is sometimes thought to be a trait peculiar to Orientals.

## ZEN DISCIPLINE

Zen teachers train their pupils in two ways—intellectual and conative or affective. To develop the speculative power of the pupil, a *ko-an* or "judicial case", which was discussed or constructed by the old masters, is given to him as an object of reflection. The teacher may request the pupil to present his views on such cases as these: "What is your original face which you have even before you were born?" Or "The object of Buddhist discipline is to have an insight into the nature of the mind, and thus to attain Buddhahood. Where, now, do you locate your mind?" Or "All things are said to return to One. Where, then, is the ultimate home of this One?" Or "When an ancient master of Zen was asked what was the essence of Buddhism, he said: 'The cypress tree in the garden.' What is the signification of this?"

When these questions are given, the pupil will try his best to solve them. He may think that the "original face" means the ultimate reason of existence, or that the "One to which all things return" is the absolute ground of things, and has nowhere else to return to but itself. According to these views, he will approach the teacher, displaying before him all his precious stock of philosophical and religious knowledge. But such demonstrations will call forth but a cold reception at the hand of the Zen teacher, though they might be in accord with a conventional interpretation of Buddhist theology. For Zen is not out to demonstrate or to interpret or to discuss, but to present the fact of faith as it is. Those who are generally addicted to talking on things which they have never experienced personally, who have taken symbols for things and intellectual representations for realities, will for the first time in their lives realize, when they are so bluntly treated by Zen teachers, how superficial and confused their minds were, and how unsteady was the foundation of their faith. They will thus, under the Zen training, learn to define their notions of things clearly and accurately; they will also be induced to reflect within themselves, as well as on things outside, from a point of view quite different from those they had held. Even if they are unable to grasp the signification of the *ko-an*, this reflective habit which they are going to acquire (though this is not the main object of Zen) will considerably help the pupils in their moral and intellectual training.

When one case is settled, another and perhaps more complicated one will be given, so that the pupil will be able to see the prevalence of one principle in all cases, and this will be continued as long as he desires.

The conative or affective phase of Zen discipline is accomplished by the means of *zazen* (*dhyana*). In this the pupil is required to sit quietly for a certain length of time, during which he will think of the *ko-an* given to him. *Zazen* can be practised by the pupil alone or in the company of others in a hall especially built for the purpose.

*Zazen* is not meant to induce a trance or a state of self-hypnotism. It aims at keeping the mind well poised and directing attention on any point one wills. Most people, especially in these days of commercial and industrial rush, are so given up to excitements, impulses, and sensationalism that they often prematurely exhaust their nervous energy, and finally lose equilibrium of mind. Zen professes to remedy this useless waste of energy on the one hand, and to increase, as it were, a reserve stock of mentality.

In conclusion, it may be of interest to our readers to see what a Zen teacher of modern times has to say about the practice of Zen, and here I give some extracts from the Reverend Soyen Shaku's work entitled *Sermons of a Buddhist Abbot,* which is a collection of some of his addresses delivered during his recent visit to America. He occupies a very prominent position in the Zen hierarchy in Japan, and is the Abbot of the historical monasteries of Kamakura, Engakuji and Kenchoji, where the Zen Sect of Japan was founded.[1]

"What is *dhyana? Dhyana* literally means, in Sanskrit, pacification, equilibration, or tranquillization, but as a religious discipline it is rather self-examination or introspection. It is not necessarily to cogitate on the deep subjects of metaphysics, nor is it to contemplate the virtues of a deity, or the transitoriness of mundane life. To define its import in Buddhism, roughly and practically, it is the habit of withdrawing occasionally from the turbulence of worldliness and of devoting some time to a quiet inspection of one's own consciousness. When this habit is thoroughly established, a man can keep serenity of mind and cheerfulness of disposition, even in the midst of his whirlwind-like course of daily life. *Dhyana* is, then, a discipline in tranquillization. It aims at giving to the mind the time for deliberation, and saving it from running wild; it directs the vain and vulgar to the path of earnestness and reality; it makes us feel interest in higher things which are above the senses; it discovers the presence in us of a spiritual faculty which bridges the chasm between the finite and the infinite; and it finally delivers us from the bondage and torture of ignorance, safely leading us to the other shore of Nirvana.

"*Dhyana* is sometimes made a synonym for *samatha* and *samadhi* and *samapatti. Samatha* is tranquillity and practically the same as *dhyana,* though the latter is much more frequently in use than the former. *Samapatti* literally is

[1] The *Sermons of a Buddhist Abbot* to which Dr. Suzuki refers is a book published by the Open Court Publishing Co. of Chicago in 1906, and includes Dr. Suzuki's translations into English of a number of addresses given by the Ven. Soyen Shaku in the U.S.A. during his stay there in 1905-6. On his death he was buried in the monastery of Engakuji at Kamakura, where Dr. Suzuki himself has lived for a great many years. It is to be remembered that this article was itself written in 1906.—ED.

'put together evenly' or 'balanced', and means the equilibrium of consciousness in which takes place neither wakefulness nor apathy, but in which the mind is calmly concentrated on the thought under consideration. *Samadhi* is a perfect absorption, voluntary or involuntary, of thought in the object of contemplation. A mind is sometimes said to be in a state of *samadhi* when it identifies itself with the ultimate reason of existence and is only conscious of the unification. In this case, *dhyana* is the method or process that brings us finally to *samadhi*.

．　　　．　　　．　　　．　　　．

"Now, the benefits arising from the exercise of *dhyana* are more than one, and are not only practical but moral and spiritual. Nobody will deny the most practical advantage gained through presence of mind, moderation of temper, control of feelings, and mastery of one's self. A passion may be so violent at the time of its agitation that it will fairly consume itself to utter destruction, but a cool-headed man knows well how to give it the necessary psychological time of rest and deliberation, and thus to save himself from plunging headlong into the Charybdis of emotion. And this cool-headedness, though in some measure due to heredity, is attainable through the exercise of *dhyana*.

"Intellectually, *dhyana* will keep the head clear and lucid, and whenever necessary, make it concentrate itself on the subject at issue. Logical accuracy depends greatly on the dispassionateness of the arguing mind, and scientific investigation gains much from the steadiness of the observing eye. Whatever be a man's intellectual development, he has surely nothing to lose, but a great deal to gain, by training himself in the habit of tranquillization.

"In these days of industrial and commercial civilization, multitudes of people have very little time to devote themselves to spiritual culture. They are not altogether ignorant of the existence of things which are of permanent value, but their minds are so engrossed in details of everyday life that they find it extremely difficult to avoid their constant obtrusion. Even when they retire from their routine work at night, they are bent on something exciting which will tax their already overstretched nervous system to the utmost. If they do not die prematurely, they become nervous wrecks. They seem not to know the blessings of relaxation. They seem to be unable to live within themselves and find there the source of eternal cheerfulness. Life is for them more or less a heavy burden, and their task consists in the carrying of the burden. The gospel of *dhyana*, therefore, must prove to them a heaven-sent boon when they conscientiously practise it.

"*Dhyana* is physiologically the accumulation of nervous energy; it is a sort of spiritual storage battery in which an enormous amount of latent force is sealed—a force which will, whenever demand is made, manifest itself with tremendous potency. A mind trained in *dhyana* will never waste its energy, causing its untimely exhaustion. It may appear at times, when superficially observed, dull, un-interesting, and dreamy, but it will work wonders when the occasion arises; while a mind ordinarily addicted to dissipation succumbs to the intensity of an impulse or a stimulus without much struggling, which ends in complete collapse, for it has no energy in reserve. Here, let me remark incidentally, can be seen one of the many characteristic differences between Orientalism and Occidentalism. In all departments of Oriental culture a strong emphasis is placed upon the necessity of preserving the latent nervous energy, and of keeping the source of spiritual strength well fed and nourished. Young minds are trained to store up within, and not to make any wasteful display of their prowess and knowledge and virtue. It is only shallow waters, they would say, that make a noisy, restless stream, while a deep whirlpool goes on silently. The Occidentals, as far as I can judge, seem to be fond of making a full display of their possessions with the frankness of a child; and they are prone to a strenuous and dissipating life, which will soon drain all the nervous force at their command. They seem not to keep anything in reserve which they can make use of later on at their leisure. They have indeed candid and open-hearted traits, which sometimes seem wanting in the Orientals; but they certainly lack the profound depth of the latter, who never seem to be enthusiastic, clamorous, or irrepressible. The teaching of Lao-tze or that of the *Bhagavadgita* was not surely intended for the Western nations. Of course, there are exceptions in the West as well as in the East. Generally speaking, however, the West is energetic and the East mystical; for the latter's ideal is to be incomprehensible, immeasurable, and undemonstrative even as absolute being. And the practice of *dhyana* may be considered in a way one of the methods of realizing this ideal.

.    .    .    .    .

"In the *Candradipa-samadhi Sutra*, the benefits of *dhyana* practice are enumerated as follows: (1) When a man practises *dhyana* according to the regulation, all his senses become calm and serene, and, without knowing it on his part, he begins to enjoy the habit. (2) Loving-kindness will take possession of his heart, which then, freeing itself from sinfulness, looks upon all sentient beings as his brothers and sisters. (3) Such poisonous and harassing passions as anger, infatuation, avarice, etc. gradually retire from the field of consciousness. (4) Having a close watch over all the senses, *dhyana* guards them against the intrusion of evils. (5) Being pure in heart and serene in disposition, the practiser of *dhyana* feels no inordinate appetite in lower passions. (6) The mind being concentrated on higher thoughts, all sorts of temptation and attachment and egoism are kept away. (7) Though he well knows the emptiness of vanity, he does not fall into the snare of nihilism. (8) However entangling the nets of birth and death, he is well aware of the way to deliverance therefrom. (9) Having fathomed the deepest depths of the Dharma, he abides in the wisdom of Buddha. (10) As he is not disturbed by any temptation, he feels like an eagle that, having escaped from imprisonment, freely wings his flight through the air.

.     .     .     .     .

"The practice of *dhyana* is often confounded with a trance or self-hypnotism—a grave error which I here propose to refute. The difference between the two is patent to every clear-sighted mind, for a trance is a pathological disturbance of consciousness, while *dhyana* is a perfectly normal state of it. Trance is a kind of self-illusion, which is entirely subjective and cannot be objectively verified; but *dhyana* is a state of consciousness in which all mental powers are kept in equilibrium, so that no one thought or faculty is made predominant over others. It is like the pacification of turbulent waters by pouring oil over them. In a smooth, glossy mirror of immense dimension no waves are roaring, no foam is boiling, no splashes are spattering. And it is in this perfect mirror of consciousness that myriads of reflections, as it were, come and go without ever disturbing its serenity. In trances certain mental and physiological functions are unduly accelerated while others are kept altogether in abeyance, the whole system of consciousness thus being thrown into disorder; and its outcome is the loss of equilibrium in the organism, which is the very opposite to what is attained through the practice of *dhyana*.

"Again, some superficial critics think that Buddhist *dhyana* is a sort of intense meditation on some highly abstract thoughts, and that the concentration, which works in the same way as self-hypnotism, leads the mind to the state of trance called Nirvana. This is a very grievous error committed by those who have never comprehended the essence of religious consciousness, for Buddhist *dhyana* has nothing to do with abstraction or self-hypnosis. What it proposes to accomplish is to make our consciousness realize the inner reason of the universe which abides in our minds. *Dhyana* strives to make us acquainted with the most concrete and, withal, the most universal fact of life. It is the philosopher's business to deal with dry, lifeless, uninteresting generalizations. Buddhists are not concerned with things like that. They want to see the fact directly, and not through the medium of philosophical abstractions. There may be a god who created heaven and earth, or there may not; we might be saved by simply believing in his goodness, or we might not; the destination of evil-doers may be hell and that of good men paradise, or, this may be reversed. True Buddhists do not trouble themselves with such propositions as these. Let them well alone; Buddhists are not so idle and superficial as to waste their time in pondering over the questions which have no vital concern with our religious life. Buddhists through *dhyana* endeavour to reach the bottom of things, and there to grasp with their own hands the very life of the universe, which makes the sun rise in the morning, makes the bird cheerfully sing in the balmy spring breeze, and also makes the biped called man hunger for love, righteousness, liberty, truth and goodness. In *dhyana*, therefore, there is nothing abstract, nothing dry as a bone and cold as a corpse, but all animation, all activity and eternal revelation.

"Some Hindu philosophers, however, seem to have considered hallucinations and self-suggested states of mind as real, and the attainment of them as the aim of *dhyana* practice. Their conception of the eightfold *dhyana*-heaven in which all sorts of angels are living is evidence of it. When the mythical beings in those regions practise *dhyana*, they enter into different stages of *samadhi*. They (1) come to think that they are lifted up in the air like a cloud; (2) they feel the presence of some indescribable luminosity; (3) they experience a supernatural joy; (4) their minds become so clarified and transparent as to reflect all the worlds like a very brilliant mirror; (5) they feel as if the soul has escaped bodily confinement and expanded itself to the immensity of space; (6) they now come back to a definite state of consciousness, in which all mental functions are presented, and the past and present and future reveal themselves; (7) they then have the feeling of absolute nothingness, in which not a ripple of mentation stirs; (8) lastly, they are not conscious of anything particular, nor have they lost consciousness, and here they are said to have reached the highest stage of *samadhi*.

"But, according to Buddhism, all these visionary phenomena as the outcome of *dhyana* are rejected, for they have nothing to do with the realization of the religious life. In the *Surangama Sutra* fifty abnormal conditions of consciousness are mentioned against which the practiser of *dhyana* has to guard himself, and among them we find those psychical aberrations mentioned above."

## LITERATURE

Zen is very prolific in writings though it claims to be an avowed enemy of letters. It has produced many learned scholars to whom we are indebted for our being able to trace every stage of its historical development. Among many books treating of the history of Zen thought we must mention the following as the most important: *Records of the Transmission of the Lamp*, which was compiled early in the Sung dynasty. It is in Japanese known as *Keitoku Dento Roku* and in Chinese as *Ching-teh Chuan-teng Lu*. Bodhidharma, who is traditionally regarded as the first Chinese patriarch of the Zen Sect, left some writings, though their historical accuracy cannot be guaranteed. They are collected under the title of *The Six Essays of Shoshitsu* (*Shoshitsu Rokumon Shu* in Japanese and *Shao-shih Liu-men Chi* in Chinese. Seng-tsan, the third Patriarch, has a metrical composition known as "*Inscription on the Believing Mind*" (*Shinjin no Mei, Hsin-hsin Ming*), and Hui-neng, the sixth Patriarch, has a book compiled by his disciples with the title *The Platform Sutra on the Dharma-treasure* (*Hobo Dangyo, Fa-pao Tan-ching*). The following two works, respectively by Daishu Yekai (Tai-chu Hui-hai, of the eighth century) and Obaku Kiun (Huang-po Hsi-yun of the ninth century), are important contributions to the study of Zen thought: *On the Essentials of Sudden Enlightenment*

(*Tongo Yomon Ron, Tun-wu Yao-men Lun*) and *On the Transmission of the Mind* (*Denshin Hoyo, Chuan-hsin Fa-yao*).

(To these must be added two most valuable MSS. on Zen which are among the Tun-huang discoveries: *Ryoga Shishi Ki* (*Leng-chia Shih-tzu Chi*), *Teachers and Disciples of the Lanka*, and *Jinne Roku* (*Shen-hui Lu*), *Sayings of Shen-hui*.)

## NOTES

(1) *Dhyana*, according to Zen scholars, is not exactly meditation or contemplation. A man can meditate on a religious or philosophical subject while disciplining himself in Zen, but that is only incidental. What Zen aims to attain is to see into one's mind and thereby to put an end to all intellectual doubts and emotional disturbances.

(2) The exact title of the *sutra* is "Sutra on the Questions of Mahapitaka Brahmaraja" (*Ta tsang fan wang shuo wen ching* in Chinese). There is no doubt that this is a spurious text. The incident mentioned here was most likely fabricated by an early Chinese Zen teacher, when the Zen was challenged by rival sects to produce historical authority in justification of its claim for orthodoxy. But this awaits further investigation.

(3) How the transmission took place among these patriarchs, as in the case between Mahakashyapa and Ananda, is related in the Chinese work entitled *Chuan-teng Lu* ("Transmission-lamp-records").

(4) In the Zen Sect succession is considered very important in the transmission of its faith. Each Zen master must be sanctioned and authorized by his predecessor, without which he represents a heterodoxy. His interpretation of the spiritual experience may differ from that of his predecessor, or he may be inclined to emphasize a certain phase of his faith which he thinks was neglected, but his authority to do so must be acknowledged by his teacher.

(5) This is a sort of loud cry, and is made frequently by Zen masters in their religious discourse. *Ho* is the Chinese pronunciation; in Japanese it is *katsu* or *kwatsu*, the final vowel of which is only slightly audible.

(6) This is one of the most noted "cases" (*ko-an*) in the history of the Zen Sect. So far as its literary account goes,

there seems nothing particularly religious or philosophical or illuminative of the Zen faith. On the other hand, the un-initiated may consider the whole affair a farce, devoid of any import, religious or otherwise. But Zen teachers think that they who understand this "case" understand everything under and above the sun. To give a typical instance of Zen teaching, I have here reproduced this incident almost as fully as in the original text, *Rinzai Roku* (*Lin-chi Lu* in Chinese).

(7) On this the well-known author of the *Heki-gan Shu* (*Pi-Yen Chi*) comments: "This 'judicial case' is very much mis-understood by some of the masters, as they do not know how to masticate and digest and appreciate it. Why? Because it is insipid and devoid of taste. Many answers have already been given to the query, What is the Buddha? Some say, 'He is in the sanctum', others, 'He is the one with the thirty-two marks'; and still others, 'He is a bamboo-whip made at Chang Lin Hill'. But Tozan's answer, 'Three pounds of flax', goes far beyond all these, and puts the old masters to silence. Those who do not understand him imagine that he was at the time in the kitchen weighing the flax, when a monk approached and asked him about Buddha, and that he gave the answer as reported. Some think that Tozan is ironical, for when he says east he means west. Some say that as the inquisitive monk, not knowing himself who was Buddha, came to Tozan and asked the question, so the master answered him in a roundabout way. Oh, these paralysed commentators!

"There is another class of scholars who say that those three pounds of flax are no more than Buddha himself. How far off the track they are! If they labour to unravel Tozan's words in this manner, they will not be able even to dream of the proper solution, though they work till the end of eternity.

"Why? Because words are a mere vessel in which the reason is carried. If you comprehend not the spirit of the master, but only grope in the dark maze of words, you would never catch a glimpse of the spirit. Says an ancient sage: 'The reason as such has no expressions, but it is through expressions that it becomes manifest; and when we know the reason we neglect expressions. Only they who have penetrated the veil reach the first fact.

"This case of 'three pounds of flax' is like the public high-way leading to Chang-An (capital): each step, up and down, is easy and smooth."

(8) A similar story is told of Mok-hyo (Mu Ping), who was

asked by a monk what was the first principle of Buddhism. Hyo said: "What a large melon is this!"

When another master was asked whether Buddhism could be found in a lonely, desolate, unfrequented region among craggy mountains, the master said: "Yes." Being further asked how that was, he said: 'Rocks and boulders there are; larger ones are large and smaller ones small."

(9) Literally, face-gates.

(10) The translation of this kind of work is full of difficulties, especially when the writer does not lay claim to philosophical accuracy. The sentences are loosely connected, and important terms are used without definition. The translator hopes that the reader will be satisfied if the general drift of the text has been made sufficiently intelligible in what follows.

# II. ZEN BUDDHISM

IN MORE than two hundred years of quiet and steady development since its introduction in the sixth century by Bodhidharma (Jap: Bodaidaruma or simply Daruma) from the West, that is, from Southern India, Zen Buddhism established itself firmly in the land of Confucianism and Taoism. Zen is proffered as a teaching which is:

A special transmission outside the Scriptures,
Not depending upon the letter,
But pointing directly to the Mind,
And leading us to see into the Nature itself, thereby making us attain Buddhahood.

By whom and when this declaration was first formulated is not known, but it was during the early part of the T'ang dynasty that Zen really began to take hold of the Chinese mind. The laying of its foundation is traditionally ascribed to Bodhidharma, but it was Yeno (Hui-neng) and his followers in the T'ang dynasty who developed it as an independent Buddhist school and a great spiritual power. It was they who emphasized that it did not depend on the letter, that is, intellection, but directly seized upon the Mind itself, which is Reality.

I propose to analyse this four-line declaration, and see what constitutes the essentials of Zen teaching.

When Zen claims to be "a special transmission outside the Scriptures", we may take this to imply the existence of an esoteric teaching in Buddhism which came to be known as Zen. But the phrase simply means that Zen is not dependent on the letter or the Scriptures, which here stand for conceptualism, and all that the term implies. Zen abhors words and concepts, and reasoning based on them. We have been misled from the first rising of consciousness to resort too much to ratiocination for the prehension of Reality. We tend to regard ideas and words as facts in themselves, and this way of thinking has entered deeply into the constitution of our consciousness. We now imagine that when we have ideas and words we have all that can be said of our experience of Reality. This means that we take words for Reality itself and neglect experience to reach what really constitutes our inmost experience.

Zen upholds, as every true religion must, the direct experience of Reality. It aspires to drink from the fountain of life itself instead of merely listening to remarks about it. A Zen follower is not satisfied until he scoops with his own hands the living waters of Reality, which alone, as he knows, will quench his thirst. This idea is well expressed in the *Gandavyuha Sutra*, the Chinese version of which is known as "the forty-volume Kegon". The following dialogue between Sudhana and Sucandra is quoted from the Chinese version (Fas. XXXII), for the Sanskrit text, as we now have it, lacks this portion altogether. When Sudhana, the youthful pilgrim, comes to Sucandra, the householder, he begins by asking him, as he asks every teacher he visits in his long and arduous spiritual pilgrimage: "I have already awakened my mind to the supreme incomparable Enlightenment, but I am not yet learned enough to discipline myself in the life of the Bodhisattva or to come to the realization of it. Pray tell me about it."

When Sudhana was impressed by Sucandra's attainment of what he called emancipation by immaculate Prajna-light, he expressed his earnest desire to know it.

Sucandra said: "A man comes to this emancipation face to face when his mind is in Prajnaparamita, and stands in intimate correspondence with it; for then he attains self-realization in all that he perceives and understands."

Sudhana: "Does one attain self-realization by listening to talks and discourses on Prajnaparamita?"

Sucandra: "That is not so. Why? Because Prajnaparamita sees intimately into the truth and reality of all things."

Sudhana: "Is it not that thinking comes from hearing and that by thinking and reasoning one comes to perceive what suchness is, thereby attaining self-realization?"

Sucandra: "That is not so. Self-realization never comes from mere listening and thinking. O son of a good family, I will illustrate the matter by analogy. Listen! In a great desert there are no springs or wells; in the spring-time or in the summer, when it is warm, a traveller comes from the west going eastward; he meets a man coming from the east and asks him: 'I am terribly thirsty; pray tell where I can find a spring and cool refreshing shade where I may drink, bathe, rest, and get thoroughly revived?'

"The man from the east gives the traveller, as desired, all the information in detail, saying: 'When you go further east the road divides itself into two, right and left. You take the right one, and going steadily further on you will surely come to a fine spring and refreshing shade.' Now, son of a good family, do you think that the thirsty traveller from the west, listening to the talk about the spring and the shady trees, and thinking of going to that place as quickly as possible, can be relieved of thirst and heat and get refreshed?"

Sudhana: "No, he cannot; because he is relieved of thirst and heat and gets refreshed only when, as directed by the other, he actually reaches the fountain and drinks of it and bathes in it."

Sucandra: "Son of a good family, even so with the Bodhisattva. By merely listening to it, thinking of it, and intellectually understanding it, you will never come to the realization of any truth. Son of a good family, the desert means birth and death; the man from the west means all sentient beings; the heat means all forms of confusion, thirst, greed and lust; the man from the east who knows the way is the Buddha or the Bodhisattva, who abiding in all-knowledge has penetrated into the true nature of all things and the reality of sameness; to quench the thirst and to be relieved of the heat by drinking of the refreshing fountain means the realization of the truth by oneself.

"Again, son of a good family, I will give you another illustration. Suppose the Tathagata had stayed among us for another kalpa and used all kinds of contrivance and, by means of fine rhetoric and apt expressions, had succeeded in convincing the people of this world as to the exquisite taste, delicious flavour, soft touch, and other virtues of the heavenly nectar; do you think that all the earthly beings who listened to the Buddha's talk and thought of the nectar could taste its flavour?"

Sudhana: "No, indeed; not they."

Sucandra: "Because mere listening and thinking will never make us realize the true nature of Prajnaparamita."

Sudhana: "By what apt expressions and skilful illustrations, then, can the Bodhisattva lead all beings to the true understanding of Reality?"

Sucandra: "The true nature of Prajnaparamita as realized by the Bodhisattva is the true cause of all his expressions. When this emancipation is realized he can aptly give expression to it and skilfully illustrate it."[1]

From this it is evident that whatever apt expressions and skilful contrivances the Bodhisattva may use in his work among us, they must come out of his own experience, and also that, however believing we may be, we cannot cherish real faith until we experience it in our own lives and make it grow out of them.

Again, we read in the *Lankavatara Sutra*: "The ultimate truth (*Paramartha*) is a state of inner experience by means of Noble Wisdom (*Aryavijna*), and as it is beyond the ken of words and discriminations it cannot be adequately expressed by them. Whatever is thus expressible is the product of conditional causation to the law of birth and death. The ultimate truth transcends the antithesis of self and not-self, and words are the products of antithetical thinking. The ultimate truth is Mind itself, which is free from all forms, inner and outer. No words can therefore describe Mind, no discriminations can reveal it."[2]

[1] An abstract from the Chinese translation of the *Gandavyuha Sutra*, popularly known as the 'Forty-volume Kegon' by Prajna, a Professor of the Tripitaka during the T'ang dynasty.

[2] See my English translation of the *sutra*.

Discrimination is a term we frequently come across in Buddhist philosophy. It corresponds to intellection or logical reasoning. According to Buddhism, the antithesis of "A" and "not-A" is at the bottom of our ignorance as to the ultimate truth of existence, and this antithesis is discrimination. To discriminate is to be involved in the whirlpool of birth and death, and as long as we are thus involved, there is no emancipation, no attainment of Nirvana, no realization of Buddhahood.

We may ask: "How is this emancipation possible? And does Zen achieve it?"

When we say that we live, it means that we live in this world of dualities and antitheses. Therefore to be emancipated from this world may mean to go out of it, or to deny it by some means, if possible. To do either of these is to put ourselves out of existence. Emancipation is, then, we can say, self-destruction. Does Buddhism teach self-destruction? This kind of interpretation has often been advanced by those who fail to understand the real teaching of Buddhism.

The fact is that this interpretation is not yet an "emancipated" one, and falls short of the Buddhist logic of non-discrimination. This is where Zen comes in, asserting its own way of being "outside the Scripture" and "independent of the letter". The following *mondo* will illustrate my point:

Sekiso (Shih-shuang) asked Dogo:[1] "After your passing, if somebody asks me about the ultimate truth of Buddhism, what shall I say?"

Dogo made no answer but called out to one of his attendants. The attendant answered: "Yes, master"; and the master said: "Have the pitcher filled with water." So ordering, he remained silent for a while, and then turning to Sekiso said: "What did you ask me about just now?" Sekiso repeated his question. Whereupon the master rose from his seat and walked away.

Sekiso was a good Buddhist student and no doubt understood thoroughly the teaching as far as his intel-

[1] *The Transmission of the Lamp*, Fas. XV, "Sekiso".

lectual understanding went. What he wanted when he questioned his master concerning the ultimate truth of Buddhism was to grasp it in the Zen way. The master was well aware of the situation. If he had wished to explain the matter for Sekiso along the philosophical line of thought he could, of course, have given citations from the Scriptures, and entered into wordy explanations of them. But he was a Zen master; he knew the uselessness and fruitlessness of such a procedure. So he called to his attendant, who immediately responded. He ordered him to fill the pitcher and the deed was immediately done. He was silent for a while, for he had nothing further to say or to do. The ultimate truth of Buddhism could not go beyond this.

But Dogo was kindhearted, indeed too kindhearted, and asked Sekiso what his question was. Sekiso was, however, not intelligent enough to see into the meaning of the entire transaction which had taken place before his eyes. He stupidly repeated his question which was already answered. Hence the master's departure from the room. In fact, this abrupt departure itself told Sekiso all that he wished to know.

Some may say that this kind of answering leads the questioner nowhere, for he remains ignorant just as much as before, perhaps even worse than before. But does a philosophical or explanatory definition give the questioner any better satisfaction—that is, put him in any better position as to real understanding of the ultimate truth? He may have his conceptual stock of knowledge much augmented, but this augmentation is not the clearing up of his doubt—that is, the confirmation of his faith in Buddhism. Mere amassing of knowledge, mere stocking of time-worn concepts, is really suicidal in so far as real emancipation is concerned. We are too used to so-called explanations, and have come to think that when an explanation of a thing is given there is nothing more to ask about it. But there is no better explanation than actual experience, and actual experience is all that is needed in the attainment of Buddhahood. The object of the Buddhist life is to have it in actual actuality and in full abundance, and this not loaded with explanatory notes.

To give another Zen way of treating this problem: Tokusan (Teh-shan) once remarked: "To ask is an error, but not to ask is also faulty." This is tantamount to saying: "To be or not to be—that is the question." This questioning has indeed been the curse or the blessing of human consciousness ever since it came into existence. A monk came out of the congregation and proceeded to bow before Tokusan, as was customary for a disciple when he was about to ask instruction of the master. But Tokusan struck him, without even waiting for him to finish his bowing. The monk naturally failed to understand him and made his protest: "I am just beginning to bow before you, O Master, and why this striking?" The Master lost no time before saying: "Nothing is gained by my waiting for you to speak."[1]

From the so-called "religious" point of view there is nothing in this or, for that matter, in the previous *mondo* that savours of piety, faith, grace, love, and so on. Where, then, is the religiosity of Zen Buddhism? I am not going to discuss this question here. I only wish to remark that Buddhism, including Zen and all other schools, has a different set of terms wherewith its followers express their spiritual experience in accordance with their psychology and way of thinking and feeling.

We now come to the second two lines of the Zen declaration: "Pointing directly to one's own Mind, and seeing into the Nature, which is the attainment of Buddhahood." What are "Mind", "Nature", and "Buddha"?

"Mind" here does not refer to our ordinarily functioning mind, the mind that thinks according to the laws of logic and feels according to the psychology described by the professors, but the Mind that lies underneath these thoughts and feelings. It is *Cittamatra*, the subject of talk in the Lankavatara Sutra. This mind is also known as Nature, i.e. Reality (*Svabhava*), that which constitutes the

---

[1] *The Transmission of the Lamp*, Fas. XV, "Tokusan".

basis of all things. The Mind may be regarded as the last point we reach when we dig down psychologically into the depths of a thinking and feeling subject, while the Nature is the limit of objectivity beyond which our ontology cannot go. The ontological limit is the psychological limit, and vice versa; for when we reach the one, we find ourselves in the other. The starting point differs; in the one we retreat inwardly, as it were, but in the other we go on outwardly, and in the end we arrive at what might be called the point of identity. When we have the Mind, we have the Nature: when the Nature is understood, the Mind is understood; they are one and the same.

The one who has a thoroughgoing understanding of the Mind and whose every movement is in perfect accordance with the Nature is the Buddha—"he who is enlightened". The Buddha is the Nature personified. Thus we can say that all these three items—Nature, Mind, and Buddha—are the different points of reference; as we shift our positions, we speak in terms of respective orders. The ideal of Zen as expressed in its four-line declaration is directly to take hold of Reality without being bothered by any interrupting agency, intellectual, moral, ritualistic, or what not.

This direct holding of Reality is the awakening of Prajna, which may be rendered as "transcendental wisdom". Prajna awakened or attained is Prajna-paramita (in Japanese *Hannya-haramitsu*). This transcendental wisdom gives the solution to all the questions we are capable of asking about our spiritual life. Wisdom is not, therefore, the intellect we ordinarily know; it transcends dialectics of all kinds. It is not the analytical process of reasoning, it does not work step by step; it leaps over the abyss of contradiction and mutual checking. Hence *Paramita*, "reaching the other shore".

As the awakening of Prajna is the leaping over an intellectual impasse it is an act of Will. Yet as it sees into the Nature itself, there is a noetic quality in it. Prajna is both Will and Intuition. This is the reason why Zen is strongly associated with the cultivation of the will-power. To cut asunder the bonds of ignorance and discrimination is no easy task; unless it is done with the utmost exertion of the will, it can never be accomplished. To let go the hold of a solitary branch of the tree, called intellect, which outstretches over a precipice, and to allow ourselves to fall into a supposedly bottomless abyss—does this not require a desperate effort on the part of one who attempts to sound the depths of the Mind? When a Zen Buddhist monk was asked as to the depths of the Zen river while he was walking over a bridge, he at once seized the questioner and would have thrown him into the rapids had not his friends hurriedly interceded for him. The monk wanted to see the questioner himself go down to the bottom of Zen and survey its depths according to his own measure. The leaping is to be done by oneself; all the help outsiders can offer is to let the person concerned realize the futility of such help. Zen in this respect is harsh and merciless, at least superficially so.

The monk who was trying to throw the questioner over the bridge was a disciple of Rinzai (Lin-chi), one of the greatest masters in the T'ang history of Zen in China. When this monk, who was still a stranger to Zen, asked the master Rinzai what was the ultimate teaching of Buddhism, the master came down from his seat and, taking hold of the monk, exclaimed: "Speak! Speak!" How could the poor bewildered novice in the study of Zen, thus seized by the throat and violently shaken, speak? He wanted to hear the master "speak" instead of his "speaking" in regard to this question. He never imagined his master to be so "direct", and did not know what to say or do. He stood as if in ecstasy. It was only when he was about to bow before the master, as reminded by his fellow-monks, that a realization came to him as to the meaning of the Scripture and the demand to "speak". Even when an intellectual explanation is given, the under-standing is an inner growth and not an external addition. This must be much more the case with the Zen under-standing. The basic principle, therefore, underlying the whole fabric of Zen is directed towards the self-maturing of an inner experience. Those who are used to intellectual training or moral persuasion or devotional exercises no doubt find in Zen discipline something extraordinary which goes against their expectations. But this is where Zen is unique in the whole history of religion. Zen has developed along this line ever since the T'ang era when Baso (Ma-tsu) and Sekito (Shih-t'ou) brought out fully the characteristic features of the Zen form of Buddhism. The main idea is to live within the thing itself and thus to understand it. What we generally do in order to understand a thing is to describe it from outside, to talk about it objectively as the philosopher would have it, and to try to carry out this method from every possible point of observation except that of inner assimilation or sympathetic merging. The objective method is intellectual and has its field of useful application. Only let us not forget the fact that there is another method which alone gives the key to an effective and all-satisfying understanding. The latter is the method of Zen.

The following few examples illustrate the Zen method for the understanding of Buddhism. Zen, being a form of Buddhism, has no specific philosophy of its own except what is usually accepted by the Buddhists of the Mahayana school. What makes Zen so distinctive is its method, which is the inevitable growth of Zen's own attitude towards life and truth.

Shodai Yero (Chao-t'i Hui-lang, 738–824), who wished to know Zen, came to Baso, and Baso asked: "What made you come here?"

"I wish to have a knowledge of the Buddha."

"No knowledge can be had of him; knowledge belongs to the devil."

As the monk failed to grasp the meaning of this, the master directed him to go to Sekito, a contemporary leader of Zen, who he suggested might enlighten the knowledge-seeking monk. When Yero came to Sekito, he asked: "Who is the Buddha?"

"You have no Buddha-nature," the master said.

"How about the animals?" demanded the monk.

"They have."

"Why not I?", which was the natural question issuing from an extremely puzzled mind.

"Just because you negate yourself."[1]

This, it is said, opened the mind of Yero to the truth asserted by both Sekito and Baso.

Superficially considered, there is no logical consistency in the remarks of these masters. Why does knowledge belong to the devil? Why is not the monk endowed with the Buddha-nature when, according to Buddhist philosophy, it is taught that all beings are in possession of the Buddha-nature and that because of this fact they are all destined to attain Buddhahood? But that we are all Buddhas or that we are endowed with the Buddha-nature is the statement of a fact and not at all the inference reached by means of logical reasoning. The fact comes first and the reasoning follows, and not conversely. This being so, the Zen master desires to see his disciples come into actual personal touch with the fact itself and then to build up, if they wish, any system of thought based on their experience.

Shinro (Chen-lang), another master, came to Sekito and asked: "What is the idea of Bodhi-Dharma's coming over to China from the West [that is, from India]?" This question was asked frequently in the early days of Zen history in China. The meaning is the same as asking: "What is the truth of Buddhism?"

Said Sekito: "Ask the post standing there."

The monk confessed: "I fail to understand."

"My ignorance exceeds yours," said Sekito.

The last remark made the monk realize the purport of the whole *mondo*.[2]

One or two more instances on ignorance follow. When Sekito saw Yakusan (Yao-shan) absorbed in meditation, Sekito asked: "What are you doing there?"

[1] *The Transmission of the Lamp*, Fas. XIV, "Tanshu Shodai Yero".
[2] Op cit., Fas. XIV, "*Shinro of the Uokoku-ji Chosa*".

"I am not doing anything," replied Yakusan.

"If so, you are sitting in idleness."

"Sitting in idleness is doing something."

"You say you are not doing anything," Sekito pursued further; "but what is that anything which you are not doing?"

"Even the ancient sages know not," was the conclusion given by Yakusan.[1]

Sekito (700–790) was one of the younger disciples of Yeno (Hui-neng) and finished his study of Zen under Gyoshi, of Seigen. He was once asked by his monk, Dogo: "Who has attained to the understanding of Yeno's doctrine?"

"One who understands Buddhism."

"Have you then attained it?"

"No, I do not understand Buddhism."[2]

The strange situation created by Zen is that those who understand it do not understand it, and those who do not understand it understand it—a great paradox, indeed, which runs throughout the history of Zen.

"What is the essential point of Buddhism?"

"Unless you have it, you do not understand."

"Is there any further turning when one thus goes on?"

"A white cloud is free to float about anywhere it lists —infinitely vast is the sky."[3]

To explain this in a more rational manner I may add that Buddhism teaches that all is well where it is; but as soon as a man steps out to see if he is all right or not, an error is committed which leads to an infinite series of negations and affirmations, and he has to make peace within. To Eckhart every morning is "Good Morning" and every day a blessed day. This is our personal experience. When we are saved, we know what it is. However much we inquire about it, salvation never comes.

[1] *The Transmission of the Lamp.*        [2] Ibid.        [3] Ibid.

A monk asks Sekito: "What is emancipation?" "Who ever put you in bondage?"

"What is the Pure Land?" "When did you ever get stained?"

"What is Nirvana?" "From whom did you get birth-and-death?"[1]

The Mind, Nature, Buddha, or Buddha-nature—all these are so many ways of giving expression to the one idea, which is Great Affirmation. Zen purposes to bring it to us.

---

[1] *The Transmission of the Lamp.*

# III. AN INTERPRETATION OF
# ZEN – EXPERIENCE

THE philosophy of Zen Buddhism is that of Mahayana Buddhism, for it is no more than a development of the latter. But the development took place among a people whose psychology or mentality widely varies from the Indian mind whose product Buddhism is. As I view it, Buddhism, after Nagarjuna and Vasubandhu and their immediate followers, could not continue its healthy growth any longer in its original soil; it had to be transplanted if it was to develop a most important aspect which had hitherto been altogether neglected—and because of this neglect its vitality was steadily being impaired. The most important aspect of Mahayana Buddhism which unfolded itself in the mental climate of China was Zen. While China failed to perfect the Kegon (or Avatamsaka) or the Tendai system of Mahayana thought, she produced Zen. This was really a unique contribution of the Chinese genius to the history of mental culture generally, and it was due to the Japanese that the true spirit of Zen has been scrupulously kept alive and that its technique has been completed.

When it is asked what Zen is, it is very difficult to give an answer satisfactory to the ordinary questioner. For instance, when you ask whether Zen is a philosophy or a religious faith, we cannot say it is either, as far as we understand these two terms in their usual sense. Zen has no thought-system of its own; it liberally uses Mahayana terminology; it refuses to commit itself to any specified pattern of thinking. Nor is it a faith, for it does not urge us to accept any dogma or creed or an object of worship. It is true that it has temples and monasteries where images of the Buddhas and Bodhisattvas (would-be Buddhas) are enshrined in some specially sanctified quarters, but the monks do not hesitate to treat them unceremoniously when they find it more useful for the elucidation of their subject matter. What the Zen masters stress most is a certain kind of experience, and this experience is to express itself in ways most characteristic of Zen. Those ways, they consider, constitute the essential features of Zen as differentiated from the other schools of Buddhism, as well as from all religious or philosophical thought-systems of the world. What modern students of Zen have to do is to make a thorough examination of Zen-experience itself and of the ways in which the experience has expressed itself in history.

2

To study Zen means to have Zen-experience, for without the experience there is no Zen one can study. But mere experience means to be able to communicate it to others; the experience ceases to be vital unless it is adequately expressible. A dumb experience is not human. To experience is to be self-conscious. Zen-experience is complete only when it is backed by Zen-consciousness and finds expression in one way or another. In the following I will attempt to give a clue to the understanding of Zen-consciousness.

Daian (died 883), the Zen master of Dai-i San, once gave this to his congregation: "(The conception of) being and non-being is like the wistaria winding round the tree."

Sozan, hearing this, lost no time in undertaking a long journey, for he wished to find out the meaning of Daian's most enigmatic statement. Seeing the master engaged in making a mud-wall, he approached and asked: "(The conception of) being and non-being is like the wistaria winding around the tree; did you really say that?"

The master said: "Yes, my friend."

Sozan queried: "When the tree is suddenly broken down and the wistaria withers, what happens?"

The master threw up his mud-carrying board and laughing loudly walked away towards his living quarters. Sozan followed and protested: "O Master, I come from a remote district three thousand *li* away, I have sold my clothing to pay for the travelling expenses, and this for no other purpose than to get enlightened on this subject. Why do you make fun of me?"

The master felt pity for the poor monk and told his attendant to gather up money enough for his return trip. He then turned toward Sozan, saying: "Some day you may happen to see a master who is known as 'One-eyed Dragon' and he will make you see into the matter."

Later, Sozan came to Myosho and told him about the interview he had with Daian of Dai-i San. Myosho said: "Daian is all right through and through, only he misses one who really understands his mind." Sozan now proposed the same question to Myosho, saying: "What happens when the tree is broken down and the wistaria withers?" Myosho said: "You make Daian renew his laughter!" This made Sozan at once comprehend the meaning of the whole affair, and he exclaimed: "After all there is a dagger in Daian's laughter." He reverentially bowed in the direction of Dai-i San.

3

In this account, what strikes one most is the disparity between the question and the answer, for as far as our common sense or logic allows us to see, no connection whatever exists between the statement concerning being and non-being and the master's laughter or, as is given later on, Yengo's repetition of his own master. The question in regard to being and non-being is a philosophical one dealing with abstract ideas. All our thoughts start from the opposition between being and non-being; without this antithesis no reasoning can be carried on, and therefore the question is a fundamental one: "What will become of our thought-system when the conception of being and non-being is wiped out?" When the tree dies, naturally the wistaria withers. Being is possible only with non-being, and conversely. This world of particulars is comprehensible only when we recognize the fundamental antithesis of being and non-being. Where shall we be when this is no more? An absolute nothingness? This too is inconceivable. Is it an error then to speak at all of the antithesis? But it faces us; we cannot get rid of this world of birth-and-death, which, however, in its present state, is quite unsatisfactory to our moral and spiritual nature. We always have the craving to go beyond the antithesis, which somehow does not seem to be final; it points to something higher and deeper, and this we wish to take hold of. The mutual conditioning of antithesis must be transcended, but how? This is in fact the question raised by Sozan.

As long as we stay with the mutual conditioning of opposites, i.e. in the world of antitheses, we never feel complete; we are always haunted with a feeling of un-easiness. Sozan must have been deeply stirred with the question of being and non-being, or birth and death, or, speaking more like a Christian, with the problem of immortality. When he heard of Daian of Dai-i San making the statement about it, he thought that there was the master who could solve the riddle and give him spiritual rest. He sold his scanty possessions and with what little he could realize he managed to travel a long way to Dai-i San. Seeing the master engaged in making the mud-wall, he approached him precipitously and wished to be en-lightened on the subject: "What will become of us, of human souls, of their immortality, when the world with all its multitudinous contents is reduced to ashes at the end of the present *kalpa*?"

The question is metaphysical as well as religious. It is religious as long as it does not attempt to develop its significance along the purely intellectual line; it is meta-physical inasmuch as its approach is by means of abstract concepts. This is a feature peculiar to Zen Buddhism. If we choose, we can call it a kind of practical philosophy, and this practicalness may well be illustrated by the laughter given by Daian of Dai-i San as an answer to Sozan's question. Sozan was metaphysically minded enough to resort to such an abstraction as being and non-being, while his practical-mindedness is shown by transforming this abstraction into the relation between concrete objects such as the wistaria and the pine tree. Even this practical-mindedness of Sozan was thoroughly upset by Daian's ultra-practicalness: the throwing up of the mud-carrier, and the laughter, and the hurried departure for his room. Daian was all action while Sozan was still on the plane of word symbolism; that is, he was still on the conceptual level, away from life itself.

## 4

As long as we are gregarious animals, and therefore social and rational, everything we experience, be it an idea, an event, or a feeling, we desire to communicate to one another, and this is possible only through a medium. We have developed various mediums of communication, and those who can command them at will are leaders of humankind: philosophers, poets, artists of all kinds, writers, orators, religionists, and others. But these mediums must be substantiated, must be backed by real personal experiences. Without the latter, mediums are merely utilized and will never vibrate with vitality.

Some mediums are more readily counterfeited than others, being subject to all devices of ingenious simulation. Language as one such medium lends itself most easily to misrepresentation, intentional or otherwise. The highest and most fundamental experiences are best communicated without words; in the face of such experiences we become speechless and stand almost aghast.

Another consideration on the subject of means of communication is that however eloquent a medium may be it will not have the desired effect on anyone who never had an experience somewhat similar in kind although fainter in intensity. Like a pearl thrown before swine, the eloquence is wasted. On the other hand, if two people have had an experience of the same nature, the lifting of

a finger will set the whole spiritual mechanism in vibra-
tion, and each can read the other's inner thought.

The Zen master is an adept in the use of a medium,
either verbal or actional, which directly points to his Zen-
experience and by which the questioner, if he is mentally
ripe, will at once grasp the master's intention. The
medium of this kind functions "directly" and "at once",
as if it were the experience itself—as when deep calls to
deep. This direct functioning is compared to one brightly
burnished mirror reflecting another brightly burnished
mirror which faces the first with nothing between.

5

In the case of Daian and Sozan, the latter was still a
captive in the prison of words and concepts, and not
capable of grasping reality at first hand. His mind was
filled with ideas of being and non-being, of trees and
wistarias, of birth and death, of the absolute and the
conditioned, of cause and effect, of *karma* and Nirvana;
he had no direct, non-mediated understanding of reality;
and this was indeed the reason why he brought himself
before the amateur mason, after travelling over a distance
of several thousand *li*. The mason master was a master
indeed in every sense of the word. He never argued with
the logician who was entangled like the wistaria round
the problem of being and non-being. He did not talk
about the absolute; he never resorted to a dialectic of
contradiction; he never referred to a fundamental
assumption lying behind the antithesis of being and non-
being. What he did was simply to throw down his mud-
carrier, give a hearty laugh, and hurry to his private
quarters.

Now let us ask: Was there anything funny about
Sozan's question? We human beings are always worried
over the disruption of things we see, especially about the
dissolution of this carnal existence, and about the life to
come after it, if there should be one. This seems to be quite

a natural feeling with us all and why should this excite the Zen master's laughter? Merely laughing was not enough; he even threw down his instrument of work, stopped his wall-making, and made for his quiet retreat. Does he mean by this that it is far better to ask nothing, to enjoy life as it goes on, to take things as they display themselves before us, to laugh when laughable objects are presented, to weep when events excite this feeling; in short, to accept all things and be cheerful about them? Or did he mean that when the world should come to an end, he wanted to enjoy the ending with the world? Or did he mean that there is no such thing as the ending of anything—things are eternal as they are, a world of relativity is mere appearance—and, therefore, that there is in reality no breaking down, no withering, thus barring all conceptual guessings based on the notion of relativity and appearance? Or did he laugh at the questioner's stupidity, which showed that the latter had failed to realize the working of something in himself quite apart from or rather along with his deep concern for the breaking down of the tree and the withering of the wistaria? Such a variety of meaning may be read into Daian's behaviour. But what is desired here from the Zen point of view is to experience the meaning itself and to leave its intellectual interpretation to the elaboration later on of the Zen-consciousness which inevitably rises out of the experience.

In any event Sozan could not take in Daian's laughter, or, as we would say, he could not grasp the idea that was behind it or in it. He next visited Myosho, "the One-eyed Dragon", wishing to be enlightened about the whole situation, in which he found himself all the more involved. Myosho, however, did not give him any plausible intellectual explanation which might satisfy a philosophical inquirer; he simply remarked that this questioning on the part of Sozan would end in renewing Daian's laughter. This was really an enigmatical confirmation of the predecessor, but, miraculously enough, it helped Sozan to dive into the significance of Daian's puzzle. The whole thing was clarified now and the only step he could take was to bow reverentially in the direction where Daian was and to express his heartfelt appreciation.

## 6

Through the whole course of this incident there are no metaphysical discussions in any form; nor are there any devotional proceedings such as confession, repentance, or mortification; again, there are no references to sin, God, prayer, shrinking from an everlasting fire, or asking for forgiveness. It starts with a kind of philosophical inquiry concerning being and non-being, which is likened to the wistaria winding itself round the tree; but the solution given is not at all along the line suggested by the question—it is absolutely beyond what the ordinary-minded people can expect on such occasions. In the whole history of human thought there is really nothing comparable to this extraordinary Zen transaction. And what is still more extraordinary and incomprehensible is the fact that Sozan, the inquirer, finally grasps the meaning of the strange behaviour of the master, which evidently solves the antithetical entanglements of being and non-being.

## 7

Somewhat similar to this Zen-incident was the experience of Rinzai (Lin-chi), whose case is given in one of my *Essays in Zen Buddhism*,[1] and I quote it:

Rinzai (died 867) was a disciple of Obaku and the founder of the school that bears his name. His Zen-experience shows some interesting features which may be considered in a way typically orthodox in those days when the *ko-an* system of Zen discipline was not yet in

[1] *Essays in Zen Buddhism*, II (London: Luzac & Co. 1933), pp. 33–35.

vogue. He had been studying Zen for some years under Obaku when the head monk asked:

"How long have you been here?"

"Three years, sir."

"Have you ever seen the master?"

"No, sir."

"Why don't you?"

"Because I do not know what question to ask"

The head monk then told Rinzai: "You go and see the master and ask 'What is the principle of Buddhism?' "

Rinzai saw the master as he was told and asked: "What is the principle of Buddhism?" Even before he could finish the question, Obaku gave him several blows.

When the head monk saw him coming back from the master, he inquired about the result of the interview. Said Rinzai sorrowfully: "I asked as you told me and he struck me several times." The monk told him not to be discouraged but to go again to the master. Rinzai saw Obaku three times and each time the same treatment was accorded him, and poor Rinzai was not any the wiser.

Finally, Rinzai thought it best to see another master and the head monk agreed. The master directed him to go to Daigu. When Rinzai came to Daigu, the latter asked: "Where do you come from?"

"From Obaku."

"What instruction did he give you?"

"I asked him three times about the ultimate principle of Buddhism and each time he gave me several blows without any instruction. I wish you would tell me what fault I committed."

Daigu said: "No one could be more thoroughly kind-hearted than that dotard master, and yet you want to know where you were faulty."

Thus reprimanded, Rinzai's eye was opened to the meaning of Obaku's apparently unkind treatment. He exclaimed: "After all, there is not much in Obaku's Buddhism!"

Daigu at once seized Rinzai's collar and said: "A while ago you said you could not understand and now you declare that there is not much in Obaku's Buddhism. What do you mean by that?"

Rinzai without saying a word probed Daigu's ribs three times with his fist. Daigu loosened his hold on Rinzai and remarked: "Your teacher is Obaku; I am not at all concerned with your business."

Rinzai returned to Obaku, who asked him: "How is it that you are back so soon?"

"Because your kindness is much too grandmotherly!"

Obaku said: "When I see that fellow Daigu, I will give him twenty blows."

"Don't wait for that," said Rinzai, "have them now!" So saying he gave the old master a hearty slap.

The old master laughed a hearty laugh.

### 8

In Rinzai's case the answer was given not in the form of laughter, but in a more forbidding manner, for he was given so many blows by the master. In fact, however, whether it is a blow or a laugh or a kick or a slap, it does not make much difference so long as it comes directly from an experience on the part of the master. Rinzai, too, failed to comprehend Obaku and had to run to Daigu for elucidation. And the elucidation came in the form of a good-natured comment: "Obaku was indeed grandmotherly!" The dealing of the hard blows was a kind-hearted treatment to wake up the spirit-weary Rinzai.

From these citations we can readily see what a remarkable experience Zen is. Is it a philosophy? Or is it a religion? What kind of spiritual discipline is it after all? Zen-experience is absolutely unique in the whole history of human culture.

To make this point clearer, I will add another Zen-incident in relation to the antithesis of being and non-being.

The same problem came up later between Yengo and Daiye, of the Sung dynasty. Yengo wanted Daiye, his disciple, to give his view on the statement aforementioned regarding the tree and the wistaria. Whenever Daiye tried to express himself, the master invariably interrupted him, saying: "Not that, not that." About half a year passed, when Daiye one day asked Yengo: "When you were with your master Goso Hoyen, I understand you approached him with the same problem, and I wish to know what Goso's response was." When Yengo hesitated, Daiye insisted: "Your asking at the time took place before an open congregation, and I do not think there is any harm in your giving me Goso's answer now." Yengo could no more refuse him and said: "When I asked my teacher Goso about the statement concerning the conception of being and non-being, his answer was: 'No paintings, no delineations can do justice to it!' When I further asked: 'What happens when the tree is suddenly broken down and the wistaria withers?' Goso said: 'You are caught in your own trap!'"

The reiteration on the part of Yengo revealed at once the whole secret before his disciple's mind, for Daiye now thoroughly understood what it was, and this fact made Yengo say: "You now see for yourself that I have never deceived you."


9


The statement that "(this antithetical world of) being and non-being is like the wistaria winding round the tree", in fact aptly describes the state of affairs about us. Intellectually speaking, we cannot go beyond this. The philosophers attempt to make it logically comprehensible —this fundamental contradiction lying at the bottom of this life—and they succeed in varied degrees only to be superseded by those who follow. Some day they may develop perfect logic or dialectic which will be the final word to our ratiocination. But people not so intellectually gifted as professional philosophers, yes, even the philosophers themselves as human beings endowed with feelings for the most fundamental experience, have an insatiable longing for a spiritual rest which may not necessarily yield to logical treatment. In other words, we cannot wait for a perfect thought-system which will solve most satisfactorily all the mysteries of life and the world; we impatiently aspire for something more practical and of immediate utility. Religion talks of faith, teaching that God somehow takes care of us, all the intellectual difficulties notwithstanding. Let the antithesis of being and non-being remain as it is; for what is beyond our intellectual comprehension may best be left in the hands of God. The faith that somehow or other things are all well with God, in whom we have our being, delivers us from doubts and worries.

The Zen way of deliverance, however, is not that of religion; to be free from doubts and worries, Zen appeals to a certain inner experience and not to a blind acceptance of dogmas. Zen expects us to experience within ourselves that the suchness of things—the antithesis of being and non-being—is beyond the ken of intellectual painting or dialectical delineation, and that no amount of words can succeed in describing, that is, reasoning out, the what and why of life and the world. This may sound negative and may not be of positive use to our spiritual life. But the real trouble with us whenever we try to talk about things beyond intellection is that we always make our start from intellection itself, although this may be natural and inevitable; therefore, when Zen-experience and other such things are talked about they sound empty as if they had no positive value. But Zen proposes that we effect a complete *volte-face* and take our stand first on Zen-experience itself and then observe things—the world of being and non-being—from the point of view of the experience itself. This is what may be designated as an absolute standpoint. The usual order of things is hereby reversed; what was positive becomes negative and what was negative becomes positive. "Emptiness" is reality and "reality "is emptiness. Flowers are no longer red, and the willow leaves are no longer green. We are no longer a plaything of *karma*, of "cause and effect", of birth and death; values of the changing world are no longer permanent ones; what we consider good or bad from the worldly point of view is neither good nor bad, for it has only a relative value. Logically, too, the antithesis of being and non-being holds good only for our relative knowledge, for our discursive understanding. After the Zen-experience, an entirely new order of things takes place, a complete change of front is effected, and the result is that a relative world of changes and multiplicities is contemplated *sub specie aeternitatis*. This in a way may be considered the meaning of "No paintings, no delineations can do justice to it".

## 10

Can we say, then, that Zen teaches a kind of mystical contemplation of life and the world? Before this is answered, let me make a further remark about Yengo and Goso, who also had a great deal to do, as we saw, with the problem of being and non-being.

When Yengo asked Goso concerning the breaking down of the tree and the withering of the wistaria, Goso emphatically declared: "You are caught in your own trap." The truth is that the Zen-experience by itself is not enough; it must be elaborated by means of Zen-consciousness or Zen-dialectic, if it is to be articulate and communicable not only to others but to oneself. The experience needs to be rationalized, as it were; it wants to speak out. It wants to assert itself, to be conscious of itself; and to do this, Zen has its own way, has opened up quite a unique one—absolutely unique, we may say. Where no paintings, no drawings can portray a perfect world of Zen-experience, how can we speak of being and non-being, of tree and wistaria, of birth and death, of synthesis and antithesis, of immanence and transcendence, of destruction and construction, of breaking down and withering and being reduced to nothingness? All these

ideas and categories are so many instruments we have
devised for our own convenience in this world of action
and work; but unless we know how to make use of them
as occasion requires, they turn against us and trap us;
that is, we are ensnared and enslaved by them. When the
Zen-experience is not properly made articulate it becomes
an instrument of mischief. The experience is a double-
edged sword, requiring careful handling, and in this
handling Zen follows its own tradition, which first originated in the philosophy of Mahayana Buddhism and later
managed to follow up the channel of Chinese psychology.

## II

I am not certain whether Zen can be identified with
mysticism. Mysticism as it is understood in the West
starts generally with an antithesis and ends with its unification or identification. If there is an antithesis, Zen
accepts it as it is, and makes no attempt to unify it.
Instead of starting with dualism or pluralism, Zen wants
us to have a Zen-experience, and with this experience it
surveys a world of suchness. It has adopted Mahayana
terminology, it is true, but it has the tendency to resort
to concrete objects and happenings. It does not reduce
them to oneness—which is an abstraction. When all
things are reduced to oneness, it asks to what this One
is reducible. If all comes from God, lives in God, and
returns to God, Zen wants to know where this God is
or lives. If the whole world with all its multiplicities is
absorbed into Brahman, Zen asks us to point out the
whereabouts of Brahman. If the soul survives the body,
Zen calls on you to locate the soul or to bring it out
before us.

A master was asked where he might be found after
his death, and he said: "Lying on my back in the wilderness, my limbs pointing straight up to the sky!" When
another master was asked about the immutability of
Nirvana, he replied: "The fallen leaves follow the running

stream while the autumnal moon rises above the solitary peak." Another appeared in the pulpit apparently ready to give a sermon, but as soon as he mounted it, he declared that his discourse was over, saying: "Fare well!" After a while he resumed: "If there is any who has no understanding yet, let him come out." A monk made an advance toward the master and bowed down reverentially, whereupon the master, raising his voice, said, "How painful!" The monk stood up and was about to propose a question, but the master cried "Ho!" and drove him out. When another monk approached, saying: "What is the most wonderful word [expressing the highest truth]?", the master merely remarked: "What say you?" Going carefully over all these *mondo* (dialogues), where do we find traces of mysticism in Zen? The masters give no hint whatever as to the annihilation or absorption of the self in the absolute, or the casting of the world into the abyss of Nirvana.

12

Mystics, I believe, generally agree with this characterization of God: "God is not an 'object' for human understanding. He utterly transcends knowledge, and everything one says of Him is untrue." " 'Be still,' Eckhart says in a sermon, 'and prate not of God (i.e. the Godhead), for whatever you prate in words about Him is a lie and is sinful.' 'If I say God is good, it is not true; for what is good can grow better; what can grow better can grow best. Now these three things (good, better, best) are far from God, for He is above all,' i.e. all such distinctions. No word that voices distinctions or characteristics, then, may be spoken of the Godhead. Eckhart's favourite names are: 'the Wordless Godhead'; 'the Nameless Nothing'; 'the Naked Godhead'; 'the Immovable Rest'; 'the Still Wilderness, where no one is at home.' " (Rufus Jones, *Studies in Mystical Religion* (London 1909), pp. 225–226.)

However mystical one may be, one cannot avoid using

the term "God" or "Godhead" or some concept corresponding to it. But this is not so with Zen. Zen avoids, not necessarily deliberately but unavoidably I believe, abstract terms. When the question arises concerning such terms, the Zen master turns them down, making the questioner realize the fact that they have no direct hold on life. Zuigan Shigen asked Ganto (A.D. 829–887): "What is the original eternal reason?"

Ganto: "Moving!"

Zuigan: "What about it when moving?"

Ganto: "It is no more the original eternal reason."

This made Zuigan reflect for some time over the matter. Ganto continued: "When you assert, you are still in the world of senses; when you do not assert, you sink into the ocean of birth and death!"

Ganto does not wish to see his disciple stay with the original eternal reason, nor does he want him to lose the sight of it. He knows that Zen is neither to assert nor to deny, that Zen is the suchness of things. The Zen masters are not mystics and their philosophy is not mysticism.

13

In this respect, Kwasan's answer, which he gave uniformly to the various questions regarding Buddha, Mind, and Truth, is significant.

Kwasan (died 960) used to quote the passage from Sojo's work, *The Sacred Treasure*: "Learning-and-disciplining is called (the stage of) Hearing; non-learning (the stage of) Approximation; and when these two (stages) are transcended, we pass on to (the stage of) Truth."

A monk came up and asked: "What is the stage of Truth?"

The master said: "I know how to beat the drum."

Another time a monk asked: "What is the first principle?"

"I know how to beat the drum."

The master's response was the same when he was

asked by still another monk: "I do not ask you about 'Mind is Buddha', but I wish to know what is meant by 'Not Mind, Not Buddha'."

"I know how to beat the drum," quickly came from the master.

On another occasion, a monk asked: "How would you treat him if a man of the highest attainment should come?"

Still the master would not give up his favourite expression: "I know how to beat the drum."

Let me note here that Kwasan was probably once a drum-beater in his career as a monk, and it is likely that not only did he say, "I know how to beat the drum", but that, so saying, he actually beat the drum, or at least he went through the whole process, keeping time, "Do-ko-dong, do-ko-dong!"

When you say "this" or "that", however abstract and universal it may be, you are singling the particular "that" or "this" out of multiplicities, thus making it one of them. We cannot help this as long as we are what we are, so many "that's", or so many "this's". The only way to escape this infinite regression is actually to beat the drum, or to dance up and down with a rice-bowl, or to sing out loudly "La-la-la!"

## 14

A nun called Ryutetsuma one day came to see Isan (died 853), the veteran master. ("Isan" is believed to be the posthumous name of Reiyu who founded a Chinese sub-sect of Zen at Dai-i San or Isan.) The master, seeing her approach, said: "Old Cow, are you come?" This is as if to say: "It is best for an old lady like you to stay home comfortably and enjoy these long spring days. What makes you leave your quiet peaceful hut? An altogether unnecessary tottering out!" The nun, however, announced: "To-morrow they are going to have a great religious function at Taisan. I wonder if you are going to attend it yourself." This is a mere story, for Taisan in the north is many thousand *li* away from Isan, which is situated in South China, and so, how could the nun know of the event and how could Isan fly to such distance? The nun seems to mean that she herself was going to be present at the function even across the great continent and that her coming over here was nothing. However old and doddering, she is mistress of herself, just as the sun rises in the East at dawn or as the cat leaps up in the garden to catch a butterfly. Can you too perform this miracle? But Isan had his own way of asserting his master-ship. He threw himself down on the floor. What did he mean by this? Did he prefer a quiet nap to the active exercise of travelling so many miles? Did he mean that lying quiet is just as much a miracle as to be busily en-gaged in the practical affairs of life? Did he mean that the absolute is active in lying down as well as in being up and doing? What was the nun's response to this? Without saying anything or doing anything, she just left Isan alone, and made for her own retreat.

What is the significance of the whole proceeding? Probably I have read too much of Zen-like thought into it. Instead of that, we may take it just as an episode in our daily life. A visitor appeared; she was welcomed and they—visitor and host—had a pleasant conversation about various things of life, among them a big feast given at a certain monastery. The old master enjoyed the visit, but, getting tired, he fell asleep, and she left without fur-ther ceremony—this is what takes place between old friends. When the event is over, we have a pleasant memory of friendship, and the matter happily comes to an end.

Shall I make a more general statement of this Isan-and-Ryutetsuma incident? We are born to this world of many incidents and accidents, we go through them doing our best, and when the time comes we say good-bye to them all. If we are bound for the Pure Land, very well; if otherwise, also very well. We are perfectly passive in this respect, or perfectly active—all depends on the point of view we like to take. Zen has added nothing to the sum-total of reality, nor has it subtracted an iota of it. Zen is radical realism rather than mysticism.

We must remember here, however, that Zen does not mean to ignore our moral thoughts, aspirations, and feelings which determine the value of life while on earth. Zen is essentially concerned with the thing most fundamental and most primary, and as to what relates to our worldly lives it leaves all this where it properly belongs. Everything that exclusively belongs, as it were, to the dualistic sphere of existence is taken up by moral philosophy, religion, political science, and other fields of human consciousness, while Zen aims at taking hold of what underlies all these phenomenological activities of the Mind.


## 15

Rudolf Otto, while referring to Fichte's mysticism together with Eckhart's, which he differentiates from Sankara's, writes: "Thus the true relationship of the man who is saved is for Fichte, as it was for Eckhart: To know that he is one with the One, life with the Life, not united but absolutely unified, and *at the same time*, to stand in this world of multiplicity and division, not straining after its dissolution, but with Eckhart, working righteousness in it, and with Fichte, completing in it the living deed of ethical culture, and thus with both teachers bringing into this very world of non-being and of death, Being and Life. He must do this in such a way that his transcendental possession is itself the very source of power and the impelling force to moral and cultural activity."[1]

Even with Eckhart and Fichte, we observe that the basis of their philosophy lies in the dualism of being and non-being, of life and death, oneness and multiplicity.

[1] *Mysticism, East and West,* trans. by Bertah L. Bracey and Richarda C. Payne (New York 1932), p. 230. By permission of The Macmillan Co., Publishers.

At times, it is true, they seem to go beyond the antithesis, but as their thought primarily revolves around the dual-istic axis, they always return to it after they have made a so-called mystical excursion into the fields of identity. Zen, on the other hand, always keeps itself in the suchness of things, where this world of multiplicity and discrimi-nation is at once the transcendental world of emptiness (*sunyata*) and non-discrimination (*avikalpa*). Zen, therefore, tries to guard most jealously against our consciousness getting tipped to one side or to the other. This is not a deliberate balancing. In the beginning of Zen-life there may be something of the sort, but the object of its dis-cipline is to transcend all such artificialities and to have the principle of suchness work out its own activity.

## 16

When Hofuku (died 928) and Chokei (853–932) took a walk in the mountain, Hofuku pointed at it and said: "Look here, this is no other than the Holy Peak itself!" Chokei replied: "Fine, just as you say, but what a pity!" Zen is loath to see its experience lopsided, for it is sure to end in a lame Zen-consciousness. Chokei's remark points to this.

Hyakujo (754–814) was asked: "What is the most wonderful fact in the world?" He answered: "I sit here all by myself on the top of Mount Daiyu." The monk bowed to him, and Hyakujo struck the monk. This striking is significant, betraying the spirit of Zen, for Zen aspires to independence, self-mastery, freedom from every form of one-sidedness which means restraint and con-ditionality.

When Baso (died 788) was asked: "What is the first principle of Buddhism?" he struck the monk, saying: "If I did not strike you thus, all the world would be laughing at me." When another monk came to him with this: "What is the idea of Bodhidharma coming from the West?", Baso told him to come forward and he would let him know. The monk as he was told stepped forward. Baso lost no time in giving him a slap over his ear and said: "The secret's already out."

When these Zen incidents are observed from the point of view of relativity and dualism, they appear to have no sense whatever; but when looked at from the inside, as it were, there looms up the big character, "Zen", which is the key to all the "mysteries" so far cited. What Zen dislikes most is mediation, deliberation, wordiness, and the weighing of advantages. Immediacy is impossible as long as we are onlookers, contemplators, critics, idea-mongers, word-manipulators, dualists, or monists. All these faults are corrected and Zen is revealed when we abandon our so-called common-sense or logical attitude and effect a complete about-face, when we plunge right into the working of things as they move on before and behind our senses. It is only when this experience takes place that we can talk intelligently about Zen-consciousness from which the Zen-incidents or Zen-dialogues making up the annals of Zen are produced.

## 17

Zen therefore is not mysticism, although there may be something in it reminding one of the latter. Zen does not teach absorption, identification, or union, for all these ideas are derived from a dualistic conception of life and the world. In Zen there is a wholeness of things, which refuses to be analysed or separated into antitheses of all kinds. As they say, it is like an iron bar with no holes or handles to swing it about. You have no way to take hold of it; in other words, it cannot be subsumed under any categories. Thus, Zen must be said to be a unique discipline in the history of human culture, religious and philosophical.

Zen often speaks of a flash of lightning as if it valued an instantaneous or instinctive action in dealing with the fundamental problems of life. When somebody asks you about Buddhahood or Godhead, you strike the questioner, saying: "What a blockheaded fellow of a monk!" There is no time lost between asking and striking, and you may think this is an immediacy, which is Zen. But the fact is far from it. Zen has nothing to do with rapidity or immediacy in the sense of being quick. A flash of lightning refers to the non-mediating nature of Zen-experience.

Zen-experience, one may say, is a kind of intuition which is the basis of mysticism. We have to be careful, however, about the use of the term "intuition". If we make it presuppose the existence of an antithesis of some form, Zen is not this kind of intuition, which we may designate as static or contemplative. If Zen-experience is an act of intuition, it must be distinguished from the static form, and let us call it dynamic or actional. The following Zen-incidents may, I hope, help one to understand what I mean by dynamic intuition which is Zen-experience.

## 18

So some more Zen-incidents are given here, in order to indicate which way Zen-consciousness tends. They are culled at random from a Zen work known as *The Transmission of the Lamp*. When these incidents are perused thoughtfully and without bias one may be able to come in touch with an invisible thread running through them.

1. An officer once visited Gensha (834–908), who treated him to a dish of cake. The officer asked: "They speak of our not knowing it while using it all the time. What is this 'it'?" Gensha looked as if he were not paying attention to the questioner, for he innocently picked up a piece of cake and offered it to the officer to eat. The latter finished it and repeated the question. The master said: "There you are! It is daily made use of and yet you know it not!"

2. One day Chosa had all his monks work in the field to gather wood. The master said: "You all partake of my power." "If so, why do we all have to work in the

field?"—This came from the monks at work. Chosa reprimanded them, saying: "If you did not all work, how can we gather enough wood for our kitchen?"

3. When Nansai visited Seppo (822–908), the latter made him see Gensha. Gensha said: "Says an ancient master: 'This is the matter I alone have the knowledge of.' What do you say to that?" Nansai replied: "You should know that there is one who does not seek being known." Gensha concluded: "What is the use of your going through so many hardships, then?"

4. A monk asked Gensha: "What is my Self?" Replied Gensha: "What do you want to do with your Self?"

5. A monk came to Gensha and wished to know how he was discoursing on the principle of Zen. Said Gensha: "I have very few listeners." Monk: "I wish to have your direct instruction." "You are not deaf?" came straightway from the master.

6. When Seppo with all his monks was working on the farm, he happened to notice a snake. Lifting it up with a stick, the master called the attention of the whole gathering: "Look, look!" He then slashed it in two with a knife. Gensha came forward, and picking up the slain snake threw it away behind them. He then went on working as if nothing had happened. The whole party was taken aback. Said Seppo: "How brisk!"

7. One day Gensha entered the pulpit, and for a while he sat quietly without saying a word. He then began: "All the kindheartedness I have given out to you without reserve. Do you understand?" A monk ventured the question: "What is the meaning of a perfect silence?" The master said: "No talking in sleep!" Monk: "Please tell, O master, about what concerns us most in Zen." "No use dreaming!" "I may be dreaming, but how about you?" Said the master: "How could you be so senseless as not to know what's what?"

19

Any reader who goes carefully over all the Zen incidents cited in this chapter will see that there is something in Zen which we never meet anywhere else in the history of human thought and culture. It certainly begins with enough rationalism since it deals, as we have already noticed, with such religio-philosophical concepts as being and non-being, truth and falsehood, Buddha and Nirvana, but after the beginning is once made, the matter is strangely switched off in a most unexpected direction, ending sometimes in what seems to be a comedy or farce or even a quarrel. Indeed, the history of Zen is filled with such records. To judge them by the ordinary standard of reasoning is altogether out of place, for the standard is simply inapplicable here. Superficial people, however, are likely to insist upon trying what ought not to be tried here; their world of vision is very limited, and they fail to realize that there is a much wider world than theirs, which is beyond their mentality. The fact alone that Zen has been thriving in the Far East ever since the days of Bodhidharma and Yeno (Hui-neng) and Rinzai, and that those masters and their followers, monks and otherwise, have contributed considerably to the widening of the spiritual horizon and to the enhancement of human ideals, is enough to prove the practical utility of Zen-experience irrespective of its ultimate validity. The only thing, let me repeat, we can state here about Zen is that it is an altogether unique product of the Oriental mind, refusing to be classified under any known heading, as either a philosophy, or a religion, or a form of mysticism as it is generally understood in the West. Zen must be studied and analysed from a point of view which is still unknown among Western philosophers, and I am sure the study will give us a rich yield, not only in philosophy and the science of religion, but also in psychology and allied studies.

# IV. REASON AND INTUITION
# IN BUDDHIST PHILOSOPHY

FOR "intuition" Buddhists generally use "*prajna*" (1)[1] and for reason or discursive understanding, *vijnana* (2). *Vijnana* and *prajna* are always contrasted.

The terminology we have in philosophy does not seem to be sufficient to express what I have in mind, but I will try my best to explain what the Buddhist idea of "intuition" is and, in connection with it, of reason.

*Prajna* goes beyond *vijnana*. We make use of *vijnana* in our world of the senses and intellect, which is characterized by dualism in the sense that there is one who sees and there is the other that is seen—the two standing in opposition. In *prajna* this differentiation does not take place; what is seen and the one who sees are identical; the seer is the seen and the seen is the seer. *Prajna* ceases to be *prajna* when it is analysed into two factors as is done in the case of *vijnana*. *Prajna* is content with itself. To divide is characteristic of *vijnana*, while with *prajna* it is just the opposite. *Prajna* is the self-knowledge of the whole in contrast to *vijnana*, which busies itself with parts. *Prajna* is an integrating principle while *vijnana* always analyses. *Vijnana* cannot work without having *prajna* behind it; parts are parts of the whole; parts never exist by themselves, for if they did they would not be parts—they would even cease to exist. Mere aggregates have no significance, and this is why in Buddhist philosophy all *dharmas* (elements) (3), when they are regarded as individual existences, are declared to have no *atman* (4). The *atman* is a unifying principle, and the idea is that, as long as all *dharmas* are conceived without any reference to that which unifies them, they are just disconnected parts, that is, they are non-existent. *Prajna* is needed to make them coherent, articulate, and significant. The Buddhist conception of impermanence and suffering is not to be

[1] For Notes see p. 124.

explained merely from the moral and phenomenological points of view. It has an epistemological background. *Vijnana* without *prajna* kills; it works for individualization and, by making each individual disconnected with others, *vijnana* makes them all impermanent and subject to the law of *karma*. It is by *prajna* that all *dharmas* are observable from a unitive point of view and acquire a new life and significance.

*Prajna* is ever seeking unity on the grandest possible scale, so that there could be no further unity in any sense; whatever expressions or statements it makes are thus naturally beyond the order of *vijnana*. *Vijnana* subjects them to intellectual analysis, trying to find something comprehensible according to its own measure. But *vijnana* cannot do this for the obvious reason that *prajna* starts from where *vijnana* cannot penetrate. *Vijnana*, being the principle of differentiation, can never see *prajna* in its oneness, and it is because of the nature of *vijnana* that *prajna* proves utterly baffling to it.

To illustrate this point let us see what kind of statements *prajna* will make when it is left to itself without the interference of *vijnana*. One statement which is very common is: "I am not I, therefore I am I." This is the thread of thought running through the Buddhist *sutras* known as the "*Prajnaparamita*" (5), consisting of six hundred "volumes" in Chinese translation. In the *Diamond Sutra* (6), belonging to the *Prajnaparamita* class, we have this: "What is known as *prajna* is not *prajna*, therefore it is known as *prajna*." When this is rendered into popular language it takes this form: "I am empty-handed and, behold, the spade is in my hands (7)." "When a man walks on the bridge, the bridge flows while the water does not."

In still another way, "the logic of *prajna*" may demand this of us: "Do not call this a staff (8); if you do, it is an affirmation; if you do not, it is a negation. Apart from affirmation and negation say a word, quick, quick!" It is important to note here that *prajna* wants to see its diction "quickly" apprehended, giving us no intervening moment for reflection or analysis or interpretation. *Prajna* for this reason is frequently likened to a flash of lightning or to a spark from two striking pieces of flint. "Quickness" does not refer to progress of time; it means immediacy, absence of deliberation, no allowance for an intervening proposition, no passing from premises to conclusion (9). *Prajna* is pure act, pure experience. But we must remember that here is a distinct noetic quality which really characterizes *prajna*, and this is the sense in which *prajna* is often regarded as an intuitive act—which interpretation, however, remains to be more fully examined.

Going back to the "staff" paradox, when the master of Buddhist philosophy produced the staff and demanded its definition, not by means of intellection, not by an objective method, the following happened: Someone came forward from the assembled group, took the staff, broke it in two, and without saying a word left the room. On another occasion, the answer came in this form: "I call it a staff." A third answer was possible: "I do not call it a staff." (10)

The staff is one of the things carried by the masters when they appear at the "Dharma Hall", and naturally they make use of it frequently while engaged in a discourse. Let me give some more examples in which the staff is very much in evidence.

When a monk asked a master as to the universality of *bodhi* (11) (enlightenment), the master took up his staff and chased him. The monk, surprised, ran away. The master said: "What is the use? When you see another master sometime later you may argue the point again." This story is not really to find a *prajna* definition of the staff, but incidentally the staff comes out and gives its own definition. The same master had another occasion to refer to the staff. One day he produced it before the disciples and said: "For the last thirty years, while living in this mountain retreat, how much of my life I owe to this staff!" A monk asked: "What power could it be that you owe to it?" The master said: "While walking along the mountain trails, while crossing the mountain streams, it has supported me in every possible way."

When another master heard of this later, he said: "If I were he, I would not say that." A monk asked: "What would you say?" The master, without saying a word, came down from the seat and walked away with the staff supporting him.

Ummon, of the tenth century, was one of the great staff-wielders, and let me cite a few of his demonstrations (12). His discourse once ran thus: "Vasubandhu, the *bodhisattva*, was unexpectedly turned into a rough-hewn staff." Then he drew a line on the ground with his staff and said: "All the Buddhas as numberless as the sands of the Ganges are here engaged in heated discussion over the Buddhist truth."

At another time, after the same gesture, the master said: "All is here!" Then, repeating the gesture, he said: "All is gone out of here! Take good care of yourselves!" At still another time he produced the staff before the congregation and said: "The staff has transformed itself into a dragon and the dragon has swallowed up the whole universe. Where are the mountains and rivers and the great earth?" Another master made this remark on the staff: "When you understand the staff, your study of Buddhist philosophy is completed."

The staff has been quite a useful and effective weapon in the hands of the masters. Though the following remark by Ummon has no direct reference to the staff itself, it may be found interesting to understand how the masters flourish it. Says Ummon: "Do you want to know how the ancient masters dealt with the matter for you? Tokusan chased a monk away with the staff the very moment the monk was approaching him. Bokuju, seeing a monk enter the gate, lost no time in saying: 'Be gone, quick! Thirty blows are coming upon you!'" (13)

"The matter" referred to here by Ummon is *prajna*-intuition, and he has the following (14) to say about it, though his discourse is indirect from the rationalistic point of view. "O disciples, do not act like this: For instance, when you hear people talk about the teaching of Buddhas and patriarchs, you ask what this teaching is.

But do you know who the Buddha is, who the patriarch is? Can you tell me what makes them talk as they do? You ask again how to escape the bondage set by the triple world. But let me see what this so-called triple world is. Is there anything that will obstruct your way in any sense? Does your hearing do this? Does your sight do this? Where is the world of differentiation which you imagine to be obstructing your freedom? Where is the bondage you want to escape from?

"The wise men of old, seeing you so troubled with illusions and hypotheses, threw their whole being before you and exclaimed: 'Here is the whole truth! Here is the ultimate reality!' But I will say: 'Here! Is there anything you can mark as this or that? If you tarry even for a moment you have already lost its trail!'"

"Not to tarry even for a moment", "Say a word quick, quick!", "Thirty blows on your head!"—all these admonitions on the part of the master point to the nature of *prajna*-intuition, and, as this immediacy characterizes *prajna*-intuition, it is mistakenly identified with ordinary intuition. This being the case, I should like to have *prajna* classified as a very special form of intuition—that which may be termed "*prajna*-intuition" in distinction from the kind of intuition we have generally in philosophical and religious discourses. In the latter case there is an object of intuition known as God or reality or truth or the absolute, and the act of intuition is considered complete when a state of identification takes place between the object and the subject.

But in the case of *prajna*-intuition there is no definable object to be intuited. If there is one, it can be anything from an insignificant blade of grass growing on the roadside to the golden-coloured Buddha-body ten feet six in height (15). In *prajna*-intuition the object of intuition is never a concept postulated by an elaborate process of reasoning; it is never "this" or "that"; it does not want to attach itself to any one particular object. The master of Buddhist philosophy takes up the staff because it is always available, but he is ever ready to make use of anything that comes his way. If a dog is near, he does not hesitate to kick it and make it cry out, in order to demonstrate the universality of the Buddha-nature (16). He cuts off the finger-tip of a little boy-monk to let him realize what is the meaning of the finger-lifting—the favourite method used by a certain master in teaching his inquirers (17). As for breaking a dish or a cup or a mirror (18), or upsetting a fully prepared dinner table (19), or refusing to feed a hungry travelling monk (20), the masters think nothing of such incidents inasmuch as they help the truth-seekers to come to an understanding of Buddhist philosophy.

As the methods of demonstrating *prajna*-intuition permit of an infinite variety, so the answers given to a problem set by the master also vary infinitely; they are never stereotyped. This we have already seen in the case of the staff. To understand the staff in the *vijnana* way of thinking will allow only one of the two, negation or affirmation, and not both at the same time. It is different with *prajna*-intuition. It will declare the staff not to be a staff and at the same time declare it to be one, and the master's demand to go beyond affirmation and negation is, we can say, in one sense altogether ignored and in another not at all ignored. And yet either answer is correct; it all depends upon whether you have an instance of *prajna*-intuition or not. If you have it, you can establish your case in whatever way suits you best at the moment. You may even break the staff in two; you may take it away from the master and throw it down on the ground; you may walk away with it; you may swing it in the way of a skilled sword-player. There are many more ways to manifest the "mysteries" of the staff. *Vijnana* cannot do this unless it is dissolved in *prajna*-intuition. There is a keypoint in all this and to comprehend it constitutes *prajna*-intuition.

This key-point cannot be expressed as a concept, as something distinct to be placed before the mind. All is veiled in obscurity, as it were. Something seems to be hinted at, but it is impossible to put one's finger on it.

It is alluring enough, but *vijnana* finds it beyond its grasp. *Vijnana* wants everything to be clear-cut and well-defined, with no mixing of two contradictory statements, which, however, *prajna* nonchalantly overrides.

The difficulty in defining the "object" of *prajna*-intuition can also be seen from the following *mondo* (question and answer), in one of which it is disposed of as *acintya*, i.e. as beyond human understanding. As long as the understanding is based upon the principle of bifurcation, where "you" and "I" are to be set apart as standing against each other, there cannot be any *prajna*-intuition. At the same time, if there were no bifurcation, such intuition could not take place. *Prajna* and *vijnana* may thus be said to be in a sense correlated from the point of view of *vijnana*-discrimination, but this is really where the root of misinterpreting the nature of *prajna* grows.

Yikwan, the master of Kozenji, of the T'ang dynasty, was asked by a monk: "Has the dog Buddha-nature?" The master said: "Yes, it has." The monk asked: "Have you the Buddha-nature?" "No, I have not." "When it is said that all beings are endowed with the Buddha-nature, how is it that you have it not?" "It is because I am not what you call 'all beings'." "If you are not, are you a Buddha?" "No, I am neither." "What are you, then, after all?" "I am not a 'what'." The monk finally said: "Can it be seen or thought of?" The master replied: "It is beyond thought or argument, and therefore it is called the unthinkable (*acintya*)."

At another time he asked: "What is the way (*tao*)?" The master answered: "It is right before you." "Why do I not see it?" Said the master: "Because you have an 'I', you do not see it. So long as there are 'you' and 'I' there is a mutual conditioning, and there can be no 'seeing' in its real sense." "This being the case, if there is neither 'you' nor 'I', can there be any 'seeing'?" The master gave the final verdict: "If there is neither 'you' nor 'I', who wants to 'see'?"

Thus we can see that *prajna*-intuition is an intuition all by itself and cannot be classified with other forms of intuition as we ordinarily understand the term. When we see a flower, we say it is a flower, and this is an act of intuition, for perception is a form of intuition. But when *prajna* takes the flower, it wants us to take not only the flower but at the same time what is not the flower; in other words, to see the flower before it came into existence —and this not by way of postulation but "immediately". To present this idea in a more metaphysical fashion: *Prajna* will ask: "Even prior to the creation of the world, where is God?" Or, more personally: "When you are dead and cremated and the ashes scattered to the winds, where is your self?" To these questions *prajna* demands a "quick" answer or response, and will not allow a moment's delay for reflection or ratiocination.

Philosophers will naturally try to solve these questions in some logically methodical manner worthy of their profession and may pronounce them absurd because they do not yield to intellectual treatment. Or they might say that they would have to write a book to give the subject an intelligent solution if there were any. But the *prajna* method is different. If the demand is to see the flower before it blooms, *prajna* will respond without a moment of delay, saying: "What a beautiful flower it is!" If it is about God prior to the creation of the world, *prajna* will, as it were, violently shake you up by taking hold of your collar and perhaps remark: "This stupid, good-for-nothing fellow!" If it is about your cremation and the scattering of the ashes, the *prajna* teacher may loudly call your name, and when you reply: "Yes, what is it?" he may retort: "Where are you?" *Prajna*-intuition settles such grave questions instantly, while philosophers or dialecticians spend hours, nay, years, searching for "objective evidence" or "experimental demonstration".

2

The fact is that *prajna* methodology is diametrically opposed to that of *vijnana*, or the intellect, and it is for this reason that what *prajna* states always looks so absurd and nonsensical to the latter and is likely to be rejected without being taken up for examination. *Vijnana* is the principle of bifurcation and conceptualization, and for this reason it is the most efficient weapon in handling affairs of our daily life. We have thus come to regard it as the most essential means of dealing with the world of relativities, forgetting that this world is the creation of something that lies far deeper than the intellect—indeed, the intellect itself owes its existence and all-round utility to this mysterious something. While this way of *vijnana* appraisal is a tragedy because it causes to our hearts and to our spirits unspeakable anguish and makes this life a burden full of miseries, we must remember that it is because of this tragedy that we are awakened to the truth of *prajna* existence.

*Prajna* thus is always tolerant toward *vijnana* though outwardly it may seem to be abusive and unreasonably harsh toward it. The idea is to recall it to its proper and original office whereby it can work in harmony with *prajna*, thus giving to both the heart and the mind what each has been looking for ever since the awakening of human consciousness. When, therefore, *prajna* violently breaks all the rules of ratiocination, we must take it as giving the intellect a sign of grave danger. When *vijnana* sees this, *vijnana* ought to heed it and try to examine itself thoroughly. It ought not to go on with its "rationalistic" way.

That *prajna* underlies *vijnana*, in the sense that it enables *vijnana* to function as the principle of differentiation, is not difficult to realize when we see that differentiation is impossible without something that works for integration or unification. The dichotomy of subject and object cannot obtain unless there is something that lies behind them, something that is neither subject nor object; this is a kind of field where they can operate, where subject can be separated from object, object from subject. If the two are not related in any way, we cannot even speak of their separation or antithesis. There must be something of subject in object, and something of object in subject, which makes their separation as well as their relationship possible. And, as this something cannot be made the theme of intellectualization, there must be another method of reaching this most fundamental principle. The fact that it is so utterly fundamental excludes the application of the bifurcating instrument. We must appeal to *prajna*-intuition.

When we state that *prajna* underlies or permeates or penetrates *vijnana* we are apt to think that there is a special faculty called *prajna* and that this does all kinds of work of penetration or permeation in relation to *vijnana*. This way of thinking is to make *prajna* an aspect of *vijnana*. *Prajna*, however, is not the principle of judgment whereby subject becomes related to object. *Prajna* transcends all forms of judgment and is not at all predicable.

Another mistake we often make about *prajna* is that somehow it tends toward pantheism. For this reason Buddhist philosophy is known among scholars as pantheistic. But that this is an incorrect view is evident from the fact that *prajna* does not belong in the category of *vijnana* and that whatever judgment we derive from the exercise of *vijnana* cannot apply to *prajna*. In pantheism there is still an antithesis of subject and object, and the idea of an all-permeating God in the world of plurality is the work of postulation. *Prajna*-intuition precludes this. No distinction is allowed here between the one and the many, the whole and the parts. When a blade of grass is lifted the whole universe is revealed there; in every pore of the skin there pulsates the life of the triple world, and this is intuited by *prajna*, not by way of reasoning but "immediately". The characteristic of *prajna* is this "immediacy". If we have reasoning to do here, it comes too late; as the Zen masters would say, "a speck of white cloud ten thousand miles away".

Paradoxical statements are therefore characteristic of *prajna*-intuition. As it transcends *vijnana* or logic it does not mind contradicting itself; it knows that a contradiction is the outcome of differentiation, which is the work of

*vijnana. Prajna* negates what it asserted before, and conversely; it has its own way of dealing with this world of
dualities. The flower is red and not-red; the bridge flows
and not the river; the wooden horse neighs; the stone
maiden dances.

To speak more logically, if this is allowable with
*prajna*-intuition, everything connected with *vijnana* also
belongs to *prajna*; *prajna* is there in its wholeness; it is
never divided even when it reveals itself in each assertion
or negation made by *vijnana*. To be itself *vijnana* polarizes
itself, but *prajna* never loses its unitive totality. The
Buddhist's favourite illustration of the nature of *prajna*-
intuition is given by the analogy of the moon reflected
in infinitely changing forms of water, from a mere drop
of rain to the vast expanse of the ocean, and these with
infinitely varied degrees of purity. The analogy is, however, likely to be misunderstood. From the fact that the
body of the moon is one in spite of its unlimited divisi-
bilities, *prajna*-intuition may be taken as suggesting oneness abstracted from the many. But to qualify *prajna* in
this way is to destroy it. The oneness or completeness or
self-sufficiency of it, if it is necessary to picture it to our
differentiating minds, is not after all to be logically or
mathematically interpreted. But as our minds always demand an interpretation, we may say this: not unity in
multiplicity, nor multiplicity in unity; but unity is multiplicity and multiplicity is unity. In other words, *prajna*
is *vijnana* and *vijnana* is *prajna*, only this is to be "immediately" apprehended and not after a tedious and elaborate and complicated process of dialectic.

### 3

To illustrate the significance of *prajna* in relation to
*vijnana*, let me cite some cases from the history of Zen
(or Ch'an) Buddhism in China.

(1) When a Zen student called Shuzan-shu came to
Hogen, one of the great masters of the Five Dynasties era,

Hogen said: "There is a saying that an inch's difference makes it as widely apart as heaven from the earth. How do you understand this?" Shuzan-shu merely repeated it, saying: "An inch's difference makes it as widely apart as heaven from the earth." Hogen said: "If your understanding does not go any farther than that, you have not got the point." Shu then asked: "What, then, is your understanding?" Hogen said: "An inch's difference makes it as widely apart as heaven from the earth." Shu then understood and bowed. (21)

Someone later added the comment: "Why was Shu wrong with his repetition? When he asked Hogen for instruction, Hogen merely repeated it and that made Shu realize his fault. Where was the trouble? If you understand the point, I will say you know a thing or two." (I wish to remark here that the Chinese original is terse and forceful but altogether loses its weight when translated. The original runs: "An inch's difference, heaven-and-earth's separation.")

(2) When Gensoku first saw Seiho (22), Gensoku asked: "Who is the Buddha?" Seiho answered: "The god of fire comes and asks for fire." When Gensoku heard this it touched his heart deeply. When later he came to see Joye, and Joye asked about his understanding, Gensoku answered: "The god of fire is fire itself and asks for fire, which is like my asking about the Buddha when I am he." Joye said: "There! I thought you understood, but now I know you do not!"

This worried Gensoku greatly and he spent much time pondering Joye's words. As he could not come to any conclusion, he finally came to Joye again and asked for instruction. Joye said: "You ask and I will answer." Thereupon Gensoku said: "Who is the Buddha?" Joye replied: "The god of fire comes and asks for fire!" This at once opened Gensoku's spiritual eye.

(3) Tokusho (890–971) (23), one of the great masters of Kegon (Hua-yen) philosophy and Zen Buddhism, before he came to a final understanding of the *prajna* way, saw many teachers and thought he had thoroughly mas-

tered it. When he saw Ryuge he asked: "I am told that the greatest of the honoured ones is unapproachable. Why is that so?" Ryuge said: "It is like fire against fire." Tokusho said: "When it suddenly meets with water, what happens?" Ryuge did not give him any further explanation, but simply said: "You do not understand." At another time he asked: "Heaven cannot cover it; the earth cannot hold it. What does this mean?" Said Ryuge: "That should be so." Tokusho failed to get the meaning and asked for further instruction. Ryuge said: "Sometime later you will come to understand it by yourself." When Tokusho interviewed Sozan, Tokusho said: "Tell me, please, that which transcends time." Sozan said: "No, I will not." "Why will you not?" Tokusho inquired. "Because the category of being and non-being cannot be applied here." Tokusho said: "O master, how well you explain!"

After interviewing fifty-four masters, like Sudhana in the *Kegon Sutra*, Tokusho thought he knew well everything that was to be known in Buddhist philosophy. When he came to Joye, he simply attended his sermons and did not ask him anything. One day a monk appeared before Joye and asked: "What is the one drop of water that has come down from the Sokei source?" (Now, Sokei refers to the monastery where Yeno (Hui-neng [or Wei-lang] in Chinese) used to reside and Yeno is considered the real founder of the Chinese Zen school of Buddhism. To ask about the drop of water coming down from the Sokei source is to be enlightened in the truth of *prajna*-intuition. Joye gave this answer: "The one drop of water that has come down from the Sokei source" (24). The inquiring monk was nonplussed and did not know what to make of it. Tokusho, who was merely present there without any desire to increase his own knowledge in Buddhist teaching, was thus most unexpectedly awakened to the truth of *prajna*-intuition. He then felt as if everything that was accumulating in his mind in the way of intellectual acquisition had suddenly dissolved into nothingness.

After this experience Tokusho was a thoroughly

equipped master in the philosophy of *prajna*-intuition, and the way he handled all the baffling problems of philosophy was truly remarkable. To cite a few instances: (25)

A monk asked: "Where does the dead one go?"
Tokusho: "After all, I will not tell you."
Monk: "Why not, master?"
Tokusho: "Because you may not understand."

Monk: "All these mountains and rivers and the great earth—where do they come from?"
Tokusho: "Where does this question of yours come from?"
Monk: "What does the eye of the great seer look like?"
Tokusho: "As black as lacquer."

Monk: "When no tidings are available, what about it?" (26)
Tokusho: "Thank you for your tidings."

Monk: "I am told that when one transcends the objective world (27), one is identified with the Tathagata. What does this mean?"
Tokusho: "What do you mean by the objective world?" [Is there any such thing?]
Monk: "If so, one is indeed identified with the Tathagata."
Tokusho: "Do not whine like a yakan." (28)

Monk: "It is said that Prince Nata returns his flesh to the mother and his bones to the father, and then, showing himself on the lotus-seat, preaches for his parents. What is the body of the Prince?"
Tokusho: "All the brethren see you standing here."
Monk: "If so, all the worlds partake equally of the nature of suchness."
Tokusho: "Appearances are deceptive."

This is perhaps enough to show Tokusho's attainment in *prajna*-intuition. In one way the Chinese language has a great advantage in demonstrating *prajna* because it can express much with its characteristic brevity and forcefulness. *Prajna* does not elaborate, does not indulge in wordiness, does not go into details, for all these are features peculiar to *vijnana* or intellection. Reasoning requires many words; indeed, wordiness is the spirit of philosophy. The Chinese language, or rather its use of ideographic signs, evokes concrete images full of undifferentiated implications—a very fitting tool for *prajna*. *Prajna* is never analytical and abhors abstraction. It lets one particle of dust reveal the whole truth underlying all existences. But this does not mean that the ideographs are suitable for discussing abstract subjects.

Tokusho's *mondo* were not always such short ones as cited above, and he often indulged in argumentation.

A monk asked: "According to the saying of an ancient sage, if a man sees *prajna* he is bound by it; if he does not he is bound by it all the same. How is it that *prajna* binds him?"

Tokusho said: "You tell me what *prajna* sees."

Monk: "How is it that one's not seeing *prajna* binds one?"

Tokusho: "You tell me if there is anything *prajna* does not see." He then continued: "If a man sees *prajna*, it is not *prajna*; if he does not see *prajna*, it is not *prajna*. Tell me, if you can, how it is that there are seeing and not-seeing in *prajna*. Therefore, it is said that if one thing (*dharma*—concrete reality) is lacking, the *Dharmakaya* (universal concrete) is not complete, that if one thing (*dharma*) is too much it is not complete either.

"But I would say: 'If there is one *dharma* the *Dharmakaya* is not complete; if there is no *dharma* the *Dharmakaya* is not complete either. For here lies the whole truth of *prajna*-intuition.' " (29)

I have digressed somewhat, but as we are deeply concerned with *prajna* let me quote another master. (30)

A monk asked: "What is *mahaprajna* (great or absolute *prajna*)?"

Seisho, the master, said: "The snow is falling fast and all is enveloped in mist."

The monk remained silent.

The master asked: "Do you understand?"

"No, master, I do not."

Thereupon the master composed a verse for him:

*"Mahaprajna—*
It is neither taking in nor giving up.
If one understands it not,
The wind is cold, the snow is falling."

I have said enough already without going back to the three instances cited above to show what is the essential characteristic of *prajna*-intuition. If it should appeal to the *vijnana* point of view or the intellect, the repetition of the statement that was quoted before would make no sense whatever. The one says: "An inch's difference and heaven-and-earth's separation", and the other repeats it; or the one says: "Sogen's one-drop-water", and the other repeats: "Sogen's one-drop-water". There is here no exchange of intellectually analysable ideas. A parrot-like mechanical imitation of the one by the other is not what logically minded people expect of any intelligible demonstration of thought. It is, therefore, evident that *prajna* does not belong to the same order as *vijnana*. *Prajna* must be a superior principle, going beyond the limits of *vijnana*, when we see how Tokusho, master of Kegon philosophy, demonstrated his originality in handling problems of philosophy and religion. He could never get this originality and facility so long as he remained in the *vijnana* way of thinking.

4

*Prajna* is the ultimate reality itself, and *prajna*-intuition is its becoming conscious of itself. *Prajna* is therefore dynamic and not static; it is not mere activity-feeling but activity itself; it is not a state of *samadhi* (concentration) (31), not a state of passivity, not just looking at an object; it knows no object; it is the activity itself. *Prajna* has no premeditated methods; it creates them out of itself as they are needed. The idea of methodology is not applicable to it, nor is teleology, although this does not mean that it is erratic and recognizes no laws. In a sense, however, this disregarding of laws is true of *prajna* because it is its own creator out of its own free will.

Thus *vijnana* is evolved out of *prajna*, and *prajna* works its way through it. From the *vijnana* point of view, *prajna* is certainly teleological and methodological, but we must remember that *prajna* is not governed by *vijnana*, i.e. by something foreign to it, and that, being it own creator, *prajna's* world is always new and fresh and never a repetition. The world was not created so many millions and millions of years ago, but it is being created every moment, and it is *prajna's* work. Reality is not a corpse to be dissected with the surgical knife of *vijnana*. If this were the case, when "the god of fire comes for fire" was repeated, the understanding would be said to have been final and conclusive, but the fact is that it was far from it and the "god of fire" had to wait for *prajna* to recognize himself in the most ultimate sense. Epistemologically interpreted, reality is *prajna*; metaphysically interpreted, reality is *sunyata*. *Sunyata*, then, is *prajna*, and *prajna* is *sunyata*.

Psychologically, *prajna* is an experience, but it is not to be confused with other experiences of our daily life, which may be classified as intellectual, emotional, or sensuous. *Prajna* is indeed the most fundamental experience. On it all other experiences are based, but we ought not to regard it as something separate from the latter which can be picked out and pointed to as a specifically qualifiable experience. It is pure experience beyond differentiation. It is the awakening of *sunyata* to self-consciousness, without which we can say that we cannot have any mental life and that whatever thoughts and feelings we may have are like a boat that has lost its moorings, for they do not have any co-ordinating centre. *Prajna* is the principle of unification and co-ordination. We must not think it is an abstract idea, for it is decidedly not, but most concrete in every sense of the term. Because of its concreteness *prajna* is the most dynamic thing we can have in the world. For this reason even the "one drop leaking out of the Sokei spring" is enough to vivify not only one's whole life but the entire triple world filling the boundlessness of space.

This miracle-working power of *prajna* is illustrated in almost all the Mahayana *sutras*, and I give an instance from the *Kegon Sutra*. When the Buddha attained enlightenment, the whole universe appeared in an entirely changed aspect.

It is evident that when *prajna* asserts itself the whole aspect of the world undergoes change beyond the comprehension of *vijnana*. This may be called performing a miracle on the grandest possible scale. But as long as the performance stays within the limits of *vijnana*, however grand it may be, it cannot be anything more than a petty juggler's artifice, for it does not mean the revolution of our *vijnana* point of view at its basis—called *paravritti* (about-face). Some think that what is described in most of the Mahayana *sutras* is poetic imaginings or spiritual symbolizations, but this is to miss altogether the main issue in the activity and significance of *prajna*-intuition.

When *prajna*-intuition takes place it annihilates space and time relationships, and all existence is reduced to a point-instant. It is like the action of a great fire at the end of the *kalpa* (era) which razes everything to the ground and prepares a new world to evolve. In this new *prajna*-world there is no three-dimensional space, no time divisible into the past, present, and future. At the tip of my finger Mount Sumeru rises; before I utter a word and you hear it, the whole history of the universe is enacted. This is no play of poetic imagination, but the Primary Man manifesting himself in his spontaneous, free-creating, non-teleological activities. The Primary Man is Prince Nata, and, in fact, every one of us, when the flesh is returned to the mother and the bones to the father. This Man, now stripped of everything that he thought belonged to him, is engaged in his *anabhoga-carya* (purposeless activity) which constitutes the *bodhisattva-carya*—a life really constituting *bodhisattva*-hood.

It is interesting to note that the Primary Man is everywhere the same but his expressions are not alike, showing marked differentiations in accordance with local limitations. In India the Primary Man acts dramatically, wonderfully rich in images and figures. But in China he is practical and in a sense prosaic and direct and matter-of-fact; there are no dialectical subtleties in his way of dealing with *prajna*; he does not indulge in calling up brilliantly coloured imageries. Let me give an example. To the monk who asks about Prince Nata's Primary Man, a Chinese master of Buddhist philosophy answers: "No mistaking about this robust existence six feet high." The monk now asks: "Is it up to the Primary Man, or not, to assume this form?" The master retorts: "What do you call the Primary Man?" Not understanding, the monk wishes to be instructed. The master, instead of giving him instructions as the monk probably desired, proposes the question: "Who is to instruct you?" (32)

While the *mondo* (question and answer) selected here carries in it something of ratiocination, I am afraid it is still unintelligible to modern man. Keisho, the master alluded to here, was not so direct as some other masters might be, for they are sometimes apt to give a kick to such a questioner, or push him away with a remark like this: "I do not know (33)," or "He is right under your nose (34)," or "Carry this lunatic out of my sight (35)!" Let me try to make Keisho more intelligible by "adding legs to the snake".

By the Primary Man is meant ultimate reality or *prajna*, as the case may be. The monk questioner knew that his individual self was subject sooner or later to disintegration; he wanted to find, if possible, something which was untouchable by birth-and-death. Hence the question: "What is the Primary Man?" Keisho was a past master in the art of teaching which developed in China side by side with the rationalistic interpretation of Buddhist thought. He knew full well how futile it was to resort to the latter method when the aspirant after the truth was really earnest in his endeavour to attain the final enlightenment. Such aspirants could never be satisfied with the logical handling of the subject. What they wanted was not a mere intellectual understanding, which would never give full satisfaction to the aspiring soul. The master, therefore, would not waste time and energy by entering into arguments with the monk who, he knew, would never be convinced by this method. The master was short in his remark, and the Chinese language is remarkably fitted to the purpose. He simply said: "There can be no doubt about this robust existence six feet high." He might easily have said "this body of yours", but he did not go into detail; he simply referred to "this robust existence", well built and of some height. As to the relationship between this physical body and the Primary Man, he gave no hints whatsoever. If there were any, the discovery was left to the monk's own devices, for the idea here, as everywhere else, is to come to an understanding by means of the inner light, by the awakening of *prajna*.

The monk in question, however, did not come up to the master's expectation; he was still on the level of intellection. Hence his inquiry: "Is it up to the Primary Man, or not, to assume this form?" This is tantamount to saying: "Is this self, then, the Primary Man?" The monk's apparent inference was that the highest being, the Primary Man, incorporates himself in this bodily existence in order to make himself approachable to the human senses. The inference may not have been incorrect as far as ratiocination was concerned, but the master's idea was not to stop there. If he had, and had given his approval, the monk would never be saved, for the point of the whole discussion would have been utterly lost. The monk was not to be left with mere intellectualization.

The master fully knew where the monk's weakness lay; hence the question: "What do you call the Primary Man?" The Primary Man was not to be identified with this individual corporeal existence, nor was he to be regarded as a separate being outside of it, as if the Man were another entity like the monk or like the master. The Man and the individual could not be considered wholly one, nothing else remaining, but at the same time they were not to be looked upon as altogether separate and dualistic. The one was not to be merged into the other; they were two and at the same time one. This undifferentiated differentiation was the point to be grasped by *prajna*-intuition.

The Primary Man is not a kind of general concept abstracted from individual existences. The Man is not an outcome of generalization. If he were, he would be a dead man, a corpse as cold as inorganic matter, and as contentless as mere negation. On the contrary, he is very much alive and full of vitality not only in the physical sense but intellectually, morally, aesthetically and spiritually. He lives in the monk's robust body six feet high and also in the master's body, probably not so robust, not so high, but full of vitality and sensibility. The monk's task was to realize this and not to argue about it. The master then put the questions: "What do you call the Primary Man? Are you the Man himself? No, you are to all appearances and in full reality a monk miserably troubled with the question as to the whatness of the Man. If so, you cannot be he. Where, then, is he?" So long as no satisfactory answer was forthcoming from this exchange of questions, the monk's intelligence could not go beyond the limits of *vijnana*, or sheer rationality.

The monk was helpless here and asked humbly for instruction. But from the master's point of view it was not a matter of just transmitting information. It was from the beginning beyond the sphere of possible instruction. If there could be any instruction, it was to evolve out of one's own *prajna*. If the monk were at all able to ask a question about the Primary Man, something of his nature must reside in the monk, and the best way to know the Man would be to have an "interview" with him by awakening *prajna* in the monk, for *prajna* is the Man. The master's role could not go beyond pointing the way to it, and to awaken it was the monk's. Hence: "Who is to instruct you?"

In spite of all these interpretations of the *mondo*, we do not seem to be any wiser than we were at the beginning. To make the matter more intelligible to the Western mind, I shall add a few words before we proceed to further *mondo*.

The body is the expression of the will, and what unites the will and the body as an individual self is the inner creative life. The body, the will, and the individual self are concepts worked out by the analytical *vijnana*, but the inner creative life as it creates all these concepts through *vijnana* is immediately apprehended only by *prajna*. When Prince Nata returns his body to his father and mother as its progenitors, he gives up his individual self, which, according to his *vijnana*, he thinks he has, and which may be interpreted as reduced to total annihilation, but Buddhist philosophy tells us that it is then for the first time that he can reveal his Primary Man or Primary Body, in which he preaches to his parents, which means the whole world. This Primary Body seated on the lotus-seat is God's creative activity. The analysing *vijnana* stops here and cannot go any further; God is its postulate; it must wait for *prajna*-intuition to transform this cold postulate-corpse into a creative life-principle.

Let me give a logical argument, hoping it will help clarify the nature of *prajna* in this field. When we say that "A is A" and that this law of identity is fundamental, we forget that there is a living synthesizing activity whereby the subject "A" is linked to the object "A". It is *vijnana* that analyses the one "A" into the subject "A" and the object "A"; and without *prajna* this bifurcation cannot be replaced by the original unity or identity; without *prajna* the divided "A" remains isolated; however much the subject may desire to be united with the object, the desire can never be fulfilled without *prajna*. It is *prajna*, indeed, that makes the law of identity work as an established self-evident truth requiring no objective evidence. The foundation of our thinking thus owes its functioning to *prajna*. Buddhist philosophy is a system of the self-evolving and self-identifying *prajna*.

This consideration will shed light on the repetitive *mondo* cited above in regard to "The one drop of water streaming from the Sokei spring" and "An inch's difference and heaven-and-earth's separation." In the case of "the god of fire seeks fire", Tokusho could not have an insight into its secret as long as his *vijnana* kept the concept "the god of fire" disjoined from the concept "fire". He had to wait for his *prajna* to come to its self-awakening in order to make the logically fundamental law of identity a living principle of experience. Our *vijnana* is always analytical and pays no attention to the underlying synthetic principle. The one "A" is divided into the subject "A" and the object "A", and by connecting the one with the other by a copula *vijnana* establishes the law of identity, but it neglects to account for this connection. Hence *vijnana's* utter incapacity for becoming a living experience. This is supplied by *prajna*-intuition.

The problem of *prajna*, which constitutes the essence of Buddhist philosophy, is really inexhaustible, and no amount of talk seems to suffice. I will give some more *mondo* here and indicate the trend of thought underlying them. Until the relation between *vijnana* and *prajna*, or that between *prajna*-intuition and *vijnana*-reasoning, is thoroughly understood, such ideas as *sunyata* (emptiness), *tathata* (suchness), *moksa* (emancipation), Nirvana, and others will not be fully absorbed as living ideas.

One important thing to remember before we proceed is that, if we think that there is a thing denoted as *prajna* and another denoted as *vijnana* and that they are forever separated and not to be brought to a state of unification, we shall be completely on the wrong track. The fact is that this world of ours, as reflected in our senses and intellect, is that of *vijnana*, and that this *vijnana* cannot function in its full capacity until it is securely moored in *prajna*; and, further, that though *prajna* does not belong to the order of *vijnana*, we have to denote *prajna* in distinction from *vijnana* as if there were such an entity as *prajna* which is to be subsumed under the category of *vijnana*. Words are useful as the culminating point in the process of thinking, but for that reason they are also misleading. We have to guide carefully our every step in this field.

In the following tabulation those items listed on the *prajna* side must be understood as such only when *vijnana* is enlightened by *prajna*; *prajna* in itself has nothing to be discriminated. For instance, *sunyata* (emptiness) or *tathata* (suchness) is not to be taken as objectively denoted. They are the ideas whereby our consciousness locates its points of reference. Whenever *prajna* expresses itself it has to share the limitations of *vijnana* either in agreement with it or otherwise. Even when *prajna* flatly denies what *vijnana* asserts it cannot go outside the *vijnana* area. To think it does is also the doing of *vijnana*, and in this sense *prajna* cannot escape *vijnana*. Even when the role of *prajna* is emphatically upheld in the drama of human activities, it must not be understood as ignoring the claims of *vijnana*. *Prajna*-intuition and *vijnana*-discrimination are equally important and indispensable in the establishment of a synthetic philosophy. In the *mondo* to be cited later, this relationship of *prajna* and *vijnana* will be noticed.

| On the *prajna* side we may list the following: | On the *vijnana* side we may have these counterbalancing: |
|---|---|
| *Sunyata* (emptiness) | A world of beings and non-beings |
| *Tathata* (suchness) | A world of clear-cut definitions |
| *Prajna*-intuition | *Vijnana*-discrimination |
| Nirvana | *Samsara* (birth-and-death) |
| *Bodhi* (enlightenment) | *Avidya* (ignorance) |
| Purity | Defilement |
| The mind (*citta*) | The senses (*vijnana*) |
| The *Dharma* (ultimate reality) | *Sarvadharma* (individual entities) |
| Pure experience | Experiences of multitudes |
| Pure act (*akarma*) | A world of causation |
| Undifferentiated | Differentiated |
| Non-discrimination | Discrimination |
| No-mind, or no-thought | Individual consciousness |
| Eternal now, or absolute present | Time relations |
| Non-duality | Duality |
| Etc. | Etc. |

## 5

The reason so many *mondo* are given below is that by going over them one after another the reader is likely to feel something glimmering between the questions and answers; thereby I can strengthen my position in regard to the interpretation of *prajna*-intuition as presented in this paper. Furthermore, in these *mondo* the relationship of *vijnana* to *prajna* is brought out in a more practical way, whereby the reader may draw his own conclusions from the *mondo*. Besides, the literature recording these *mondo* is generally inaccessible to Western readers, and it seems appropriate to make use of this opportunity to quote them for the benefit of those who are interested in the subject. There is an almost inexhaustible mine of *mondo* in China and Japan, and there is no reason for it to remain unexplored.

The subjects of the *mondo* are varied; they appear sometimes not at all concerned with topics of Buddhist philosophy because they deal with such subjects as "one standing at the head of a ridge ten thousand feet high", "the master of a monastery", "the place where a monk comes from", "a tombstone showing no seams", "the moon on a cloudless night", "playing on a stringless harp", and so on. As to the answers given even to the highest ideas of philosophy and religion, they are treated with the utmost indifference, as we can see in many of the *mondo* that follow. To those who have never been initiated into this mysterious world of Buddhist philosophy, the *mondo* will surely be a cache of absurdities. But from the Buddhist point of view there are no methods more effective than the *mondo* for demonstrating the specific character of *prajna*-intuition.

Let us start, then, with the problem of the Self.

Sekito (700–790) (36) was one of the greatest figures in the Buddhism of the T'ang dynasty. A monk called Shiri once asked him: "What is that which makes up this Self?" To this the master answered, in the form of a counter-question: "What do you want from me?"

The monk said: "If I do not ask you, where can I get the solution?"

"Did you ever lose it?" concluded the master.

Bunsui of Hoji monastery in Kinryo gave this discourse to his monks:

"O monks, you have been here for some time, the winter session is over and the summer is come. Have you had an insight into your Self, or not? If you have, let me be your witness, so that you will have a right view and not be led by wrong views."

A monk came forward and asked: "What is my Self?"

The master answered: "What a fine specimen of manhood with a pair of bright eyes!" (37)

Yentoku of Yentsu-in monastery: (38)
Q. "What is my Self?"
A. "What makes you specifically ask this question?"

Ki of Unryu-in monastery: (39)
Q. "What is my Self?"
A. "It is like you and me."
Q. "In this case there is no duality."
A. "Eighteen thousand miles off!"

Yo of Kori monastery: (40)
Q. "When I lack clear insight into my own Self, what shall I do?"
A. "No clear insight."
Q. "Why not?"
A. "Don't you know that it's one's own business?"

Kaitotsu of Tozen monastery: (41)
Q. "I have not yet clearly seen into my own nature. May I be instructed by you?"
A. "Why are you not thankful for it?"

Tokuichi of Ryugeji monastery: (42)
Q. "What is my Self?"
A. "You are putting frost on top of snow."

Various answers are given to this question: "What is the Self?" They are so various, indeed, that one fails to find a common denominator whereby they yield a uniform solution. The answer requires certain insight into what constitutes the Self, and this cannot be attained by merely thinking it over intellectually. While thinking is needed, what solves the question is not, after all, the intellect but the will power. It is solved by an existential method, and not by abstraction or by postulation. Buddhist philosophy is built upon the most fundamental, pre-rationalistic *prajna*-intuition. When this is reached, such problems as the Self, ultimate reality, the Buddha-*dharma*, the Tao, the Source, the Mind, etc., are all solved. However infinitely variable the master's ways of handling them may be, there is always one line of approach whereby they become intelligible.

To of Kokutai monastery: (43)
Q. "When the old mirror is not yet polished, what would you say of it?"
A. "The old mirror."
Q. "When it is polished, what of it?"
A. "The old mirror."

The "old mirror" is another name for the Self in a state of undifferentiation. "Polished" means differentiation. The "old mirror" remains the same whether or not it is differentiated.

A monk asked Chikaku of Yomyo monastery: (44)
"What is the great perfect mirror?"
"An old broken tray!" was the answer.

In this "the mirror" is not even an "old one"; it is an old broken tray, altogether useless. Zen philosophers of Buddhism often use this kind of expression when they wish to show the utter worthlessness of a concept where *prajna*-intuition is concerned.

Doke of Byakuryu-in monastery: (45)

Q. "What is the Tao?"

A. "The rider on the donkey sees the donkey."

Ryoku of Tozen-in monastery: (46)

Q. "What is the Tao?"

A. "This, right here!"

Juten of Hofuku-in monastery: (47)

Q. "I am told that when one wishes to attain the way of the Unborn, one must see into the Source. What is the Source?"

The master remained silent for a while, and then asked the attendant: "What did that monk ask me just now?" The monk repeated the question, which made the master scoff at him, saying: "I am not deaf!"

Juten (47), the master, once asked a monk: "Where do you come from?"

The monk answered: "I come from a monastery on the western side of the river where Kwannon is enshrined."

The master said: "Did you see Kwannon?"

"Yes, I did."

"Did you see it on the right side or the left side?"

The monk replied: "When seeing there is neither right nor left."

In a *mondo* like this, one can readily see that the question at issue is not Kwannon, which is used merely as a symbol for the Self, or the Tao, or ultimate reality, and the seeing of it means *prajna*-intuition. There is no differentiation in it of right and left; it is complete in itself; it is a unity in itself; it is "pure" seeing. This monk apparently understood what *prajna*-intuition was, and this form of question on the part of the master is known as a "trial" question.

Juten (47), the master, saw the head cook and asked: "How large is your cooking pan?"

The monk cook said: "You measure it yourself and see."

The master assumed the position of measuring it with his hands.

The monk remarked: "Do not make a fool of me."
The master retorted: "It is you who are making a fool of me."

The master (47), once seeing a monk, remarked: 'How did you manage to be so tall as that?"
The monk answered: "How short are you?"
The master crouched as if making himself shorter.
The monk said: "Do not make a fool of me, O master!"
The master retorted: "It is you who are making a fool of me!"

Goshin of Saikoji monastery: (48)
Q. "What is the *mani*-jewel that takes colours?"
A. "Blue, yellow, red and white."
Q. "What is the *mani*-jewel that does not take colours?"
A. "Blue, yellow, red and white."

The *mani*-jewel is also symbolic, as is evident. The *mani*-jewel that takes colours refers to reality, or *sunyata*, conceived as subject to differentiation, while the *mani*-jewel that does not take colours is reality itself. The master's answers, however, are the same to both questions; apparently he makes no distinction between the two. Intellectually or conceptually, there is decidedly a distinction, which is ignored by *prajna*-intuition. Another master, who may wish to make his inquirers see another phase of *prajna*-intuition, is likely to give his answers quite a different colour. This is instanced by the *mondo* of the "old mirror".

Shototsu of Jaran monastery: (49)
Q. "Who is the Buddha?"
A. "Whom are you asking?"

Fukusen: (50)
Q. "Who is the Buddha?"
A. "I do not know."

Reikan of Korea: (51)
Q. "Who is the Buddha?"
A. "Carry this lunatic away from here!"

Kin of Koken monastery: (52)
Q. "Who is the Buddha?"
A. "Right under your nose."

Kyoyu of Hoju monastery: (53)
Q. "What is the ultimate principle of Buddhism?"
A. "Come nearer."
The monk moved forward, and the master said: "Do you understand?"
The monk said: "I do not, master."
The master remarked: "It is like a flash of lightning, and it went æons ago."

Chikaku of Yomyoji: (54)
A monk said: "I am told that all Buddhas and all the Buddha-*dharmas* issue from one *sutra*. What could this *sutra* be?"
The master replied: "Revolving on for ever; no checking it, and no arguing, no talking can catch it." (55)
Q. "How shall I then receive and hold it?"
A. "If you wish to receive and hold it, you should hear it with your *eyes*."

Soton of Dairin monastery: (56)
A monk asked: "How do we discourse on the highest truth of Buddhist philosophy?"
To this Gensha, the master, answered: "Few hear it."
The monk later came to Soton and asked: "What did Gensha mean?"
Soton said: "When you have finished removing Mt. Sekiji, I will tell you." (57)
Jyu of Kisu monastery later commented on this:
"Speak low, please."

This interjection of comment by the later masters on a *mondo*, which took place between their predecessors and the questioners, is quite common. It is not necessarily a criticism, but is directed toward bringing out what is implied in the *mondo*. Gensha said: "Few hear it," and Jyu, referring to it, said: "Speak low!" The masters are generally off the track of "logic", and they frequently indulge in making fun of one another. They are witty and sportive. Followers of *prajna*-intuition naturally avoid getting into a philosophical discussion of abstract ideas; they are partial to figures, imageries, facts of daily experience. The following, picked at random from numerous such examples, will show what I mean here.

A monk asked Zembi of Shurei monastery: (58)
"I understand that all the rivers, however different their sources, pour into the great ocean. How many drops of water could there be in the ocean?"

The master asked: "Have you ever been to the ocean?"

Monk: "What then, after we have been to the ocean?"

The master replied: "You come tomorrow and I will tell you."

The monk who asked about the ocean evidently knows something about Buddhist philosophy; hence his second question: "What after having been there?" Seeing this, the master retorts: "Come tomorrow." They both understand, and the *mondo* serves to give us insight into the nature of *prajna*-intuition. One may ask: "What has the ocean to do with *prajna*?" But the ocean here referred to is the ocean of *sunyata*, in which all the phenomenal world is absorbed, and the counting of drops of water in it is to understand what becomes of the multiplicity absorbed therein. The monk wants to find out what the master will say concerning the relationship between the one and the many, between *prajna* and *vijnana*. To apprehend this no amount of philosophical argument helps, leading only to further confusion, and the expected "tomorrow" will never come. Instead of indulging in epistemological methodology, "I do not know" sums up the essence of *prajna*-intuition.

Seishu of Rinninji monastery: (59)
He once asked a monk: "Do you understand the Buddha-*dharma* (the truth or ultimate reality)?"

The monk said: "No, I do not, master."

"You honestly do not?"

"That is right, master."

"You leave me now and come tomorrow."
The monk bowed saying: "Fare thee well."
The master then said: "No, that is not the point."

This "come tomorrow" was taken by the monk in its
literal or intellectual sense, and to remind him of his misunderstanding the master soft-heartedly states: "That is
not the point." The point is to understand what is not
understandable, to know what is unknowable, wherein
*prajna*-intuition really consists.

A monk asked Yomyo (60): "I have been with you for a
long time, and yet I am unable to understand your way. How
is this?"
The master said: "Where you do not understand, there is
the point for your understanding."
"How is any understanding possible where it is
impossible?"
The master said: "The cow gives birth to a baby elephant;
clouds of dust rise over the ocean."

When Seishu (61) was still in his novitiate stage under
Joye, the latter, pointing at the rain, remarked: "Every drop
of it fills your eyes."
Seishu at the time failed to understand this, but afterwards,
while studying the *Avatamsaka Sutra*, the meaning dawned on
him. Later, in one of his discourses, he said: "All the Buddhas
in the ten quarters of the world are ever facing you. Do you
see them? If you say you see, do you see them with the mind
or with the eye?"
On another occasion this was his discourse: "It is said that
when one sees form (*rupa*) one sees mind (*citta*). Let me ask
you, what do you call the mind? The mountains and rivers
and the great earth extending before you—this world of
pluralities—blue and yellow, red and white, men and women,
etc., infinitely varying in forms—are they mind, or are they
not mind? If they are the mind, how does it transform itself
into an infinite number of things? If they are not the mind,
why is it said that when you see form you see the mind? Do
you understand?
"Just because you fail to grasp this point and go on
cherishing your confused views in manifold ways, you

erroneously see differences and unities where there are really
no differences and no unities.

"Just at this very moment your immediate apprehension
of the mind is imperative, and then you will realize that it is
vast emptiness and there is nothing to see, nothing to hear. . . ."

This idea of "vast emptiness" is quite puzzling and
baffling and always tends to be understood from the
relative point of view. Buddhist philosophy has *sat* for
"being", *asat* for "non-being", and *sunyata* for "emptiness",
showing that "emptiness" has a positive connotation and
is not a mere negation. *Sunyata* transcends being and non-
being; that is, both presuppose the idea of *sunyata*. Therefore, when a Buddhist philosopher declares that there is
nothing to see, nothing to hear, etc., we must understand
it as not denying the experiences of our daily life but as
indeed confirming them in every way. Hence the following:

Keijyu of Hannya monastery (62) came to the "Dharma-
Hall" and the monks congregated, hearing the board struck
three times, which was the signal for them to come together.
The master then recited an impromptu verse:

"Strange indeed—the board thrice struck,
And you monks are all gathered here.
As you already know well how to tell the time,
I need not repeat it over again."

He left the hall without saying anything further.

Buddhist philosophers, including every one of us ordinary sentient beings, not only hear sounds and see
flowers, but also offer flowers to the Buddha, burn incense
before him, and perform all kinds of acts of religious piety.
We may not all claim to be Buddhists; we may even
protest against being called religious; but the deeds here
mentioned are what we are performing every day. It does
not make any difference whether we are Buddhists or
Christians or communists.

Muhaki of Suibi monastery (63) was a disciple of Tanka (64). When he was found one day offering food to the *arhats* (65) a monk remarked: "Tanka burned the wooden image of the Buddha, and you offer food to the wooden *arhats*. How is that?"

Suibi said: "Let him burn the Buddha if he wants to, but he can never burn the Buddha to ashes. As for myself, I just offer this to the *arhats*."

There was another monk, who said this: "As to offering food to the *arhats*, do they come to partake it?"

Suibi said: "Do you eat every day, O monk?"

The monk made no answer. The master's comment was: "Few indeed are the intelligent!"

To conclude this section, let me add a word in regard to the distinction between *prajna* and *vijnana* in the understanding of the *mondo*. *Vijnana* has a methodology, but *prajna* has none because it always demands immediacy and never allows hesitation or reflection in any form. When you see a flower, you know at once that it is a flower. When you dip your hand in cold water, you realize that it is cold, and this immediately, not after a moment of reflection. In this respect *prajna*-intuition is like perception. The difference between the two is that perception does not go beyond the senses whereas intuition is far more deeply seated. When perception touches this foundation, it becomes *prajna*-intuition. For perception to develop into *prajna*, something must be added to it. This added something, however, is not something added from outside; it is the perception itself, and to realize this is the function of *prajna*-intuition. In other words, this is *prajna* intuiting itself; *prajna* is its own methodology.

When I draw a line on paper, it is not at all straight, but I can use it geometrically as such and demonstrate all the properties belonging to it. As far as visual perception is concerned the line is limited, but, when our geometrical conception of a straight line is added to it, we can make it function as such. In a similar way, *prajna*-intuition in one case makes the "rock nod even before the master uttered a word" (66), and in another case

keeps the master very much alive even after he is cremated
and his bones sound like copper. "How?" one may ask,
in this second case. The master would say: "Does not the
boy-attendant respond to my call, saying: 'Yes, master'?"
One might still insist that the boy is not the master. If
I were the master I might strike you down, saying: "No
such nonsense, O you stupid fellow!" But as I am not, I
will say instead: "Your vision is still beclouded by *vijnana*.
You see the master on one side and the boy on the other,
keeping them separate according to our so-called objective
method of interpreting an experience. You do not see
them living in each other, and you fail to perceive that
death 'objectively' comes to the master but has no power
over 'that' which makes the boy respond to the master's
call. To see this 'that' is *prajna*-intuition."

6

This "that" is what is primarily and immediately
given to our consciousness. It may be called "undifferentiated continuum", to use Mr. Northrop's term. To
the Western mind, "continuum" may be better than *sunyata*, though it is likely to be misinterpreted as something
"objectively" existing and apprehensible by *vijnana*. In
the "continuum" immediately given, however, there is
no differentiation of subject and object, of the seer and
the seen. It is the "old mirror" that has not yet been
polished, and therefore no world of multiplicities is reflected in the "mirror". It is the Primary Man, in whom
neither flesh nor bones are left and yet who can reveal
himself not only to his parents but to all his brothers, non-
sentient as well as sentient. It is "the father" whose age
is not calculable by means of numbers and therefore to
whom everything is a "grandchild" of conceptualization.
It lives with *prajna* in the absolute state of quiescence, in
which no polarization has taken place. It therefore eludes
our efforts to bring it out to the discriminable surface of
consciousness. We cannot speak of it as "being" or as

"non-being". The categories created by ratiocination are not at all applicable here. If we attempt to wake it from the eternal silence of "*neti, neti*" (not this, not this) we "murder" it, and what *vijnana* perceives is a most mercilessly mutilated corpse.

*Prajna* abides here, but it is never awakened by itself. When it is awakened it is always by *vijnana*. *Vijnana*, however, does not realize this fact, for *vijnana* always imagines that without *vijnana* there is no experienceable world, that if *prajna* belongs in this world it must be of the same order as *vijnana*, and therefore that *prajna* can well be dispensed with. But the fact is that *vijnana* is never *vijnana* without *prajna*; *prajna* is the necessary postulate of *vijnana*; it is what makes the law of identity workable, and this law is the foundation of *vijnana*. *Vijnana* is not the creator of the logical law, but it works by means of the law. *Vijnana* takes it as something given and not provable by any means devised by *vijnana*, for *vijnana* itself is conditioned by it. The eye cannot see itself; to do this a mirror is needed, but what it sees is not itself, only its reflection. *Vijnana* may devise some means to recognize itself, but the recognition turns out to be conceptual, as something postulated.

*Prajna*, however, is the eye that can turn itself within and see itself, because it is the law of identity itself. It is due to *prajna* that subject and object become identifiable, and this is done without mediation of any kind. *Vijnana* always needs mediation as it moves on from one concept to another—this is in the very nature of *vijnana*. But *prajna*, being the law of identity itself, demands no transferring from subject to object. Therefore, it swings the staff; sometimes it asserts; sometimes it negates, and declares that "A is not-A and therefore A is A". This is the "logic" of *prajna*-intuition. The "undifferentiated continuum" is to be understood in this light.

When the "undifferentiated continuum" is the outcome of *vijnana* dialectics, it remains a concept and never an experience. Buddhist philosophy, on the contrary, starts from pure experience, from self-identity, as self-evolving and self-discriminating activity, and *vijnana* comes into existence. In *vijnana*, therefore, there is always the potentiality of *prajna*-intuition. When a flower is perceived as an object in the world of multiplicity, we recognize *vijnana* functioning and along with it *prajna*-intuition. But, as most of us stop at *vijnana* and fail to reach *prajna*, our vision becomes limited and does not penetrate deeply enough to reach ultimate reality or *sunyata*. So, it is declared that the unenlightened do not see the real flower in the light of suchness (*tathata*). From *vijnana* to *prajna* is not a continuous process or progress. If it were, *prajna* would cease to be *prajna*; it would become another form of *vijnana*. There is a gap between the two; no transition is possible; hence there is a leap, "an existential leap". From *vijnana*-thinking to *prajna*-seeing there is no mediating concept, no room for intellection, no time for deliberation. So, the Buddhist master urges us to "speak quick, quick!" Immediacy, no interpretation, no explanatory apology—this is what constitutes *prajna*-intuition.

I stated at the beginning that *prajna* takes in the whole, while *vijnana* is concerned with parts. This needs to be explained in more detail. If parts are mere aggregates, unconnected and incoherent masses, *vijnana* cannot make them the subject of intellectual analysis. The reason *vijnana* can deal with parts is that these parts are related to the whole, individually and collectively, and as such they present themselves to *vijnana*. Each unit (or monad) is associated with another unit singly and with all other units collectively in a net-like fashion. When one is taken up all the rest follow it. *Vijnana* understands this and can trace the intricacy of relationship existing among them and state that there must be an integrating principle underlying them. Not only this, but *vijnana* can also formulate what such principles are, as is done by philosophy and science. But *vijnana* cannot do this over the entire field of realities; its vision is limited to limited areas, which cannot be extended indefinitely. They have to halt somewhere.

*Prajna's* vision, however, knows no bounds; it includes the totality of things, not as a limited continuum, but as going beyond the boundlessness of space and the endlessness of time. *Prajna* is a unifying principle. It does this not by going over each individual unit as belonging to an integrated whole but by apprehending the latter at one glance, as it were. While the whole is thus apprehended, the parts do not escape from entering into this vision by *prajna*. We can better describe this experience as the self-evolution of *prajna* whereby the whole is conceived dynamically and not statically.

The continuum is not to be interpreted as merely an accumulation of units or monads; it is not a notion reached by adding one unit to another and repeating the process indefinitely. It is a concrete, indivisible, undefinable whole. In it there is no differentiation of parts and whole. It is, as Zen Buddhist philosophers would say, "an iron bar of ten thousand miles"; it has no "hole" by which it can be grasped. It is "dark"; no colours are discernible here. It is like a bottomless abyss where there is nothing discriminable as subject and object. These statements, we may say, are figurative and do not give much information regarding *prajna*-intuition. But to those who have gone through the actual experience of *prajna*-intuition these figurative, symbolic descriptions are really significant. What is asked of the professional philosopher is to translate them into his terminology according to the technique he uses.

It is evident that the continuum is not the whole attained by the accumulation of units; to be the whole, then, there must be something added to it, and this is what is done by *prajna*-intuition. Therefore, *prajna* must be considered a value-giving principle. When *prajna* goes through the continuum the whole thing acquires a value and every part of it becomes significant and pulsates with life-blood. Each unit, even the most insignificant part, now appears in a new situation, full of meaning. A blade of grass is not something to be trodden under one's feet as standing in no relation to the whole. A grain of rice inadvertently dropped off the washing pail is truly the root from which the ten thousand things germinate. This is why it is said that *prajna* vivifies while *vijnana* kills. Parts are to be united in the whole to become significant, and this kind of unification, not mechanical or arithmetical, is the doing of *prajna*-intuition. *Vijnana* realizes this only when it is infused with *prajna*.

When we speak of the *prajna*-continuum as undifferentiated or differentiated, we must not think that this process of differentiation is a function given to the continuum from an outside source. The differentiation is evolved from within the continuum, for it is not the nature of the *prajna*-continuum to remain in a state of *sunyata*, absolutely motionless. It demands of itself that it differentiate itself unlimitedly, and at the same time it desires to remain itself. *Prajna* is always trying to preserve its self-identity and yet subjects itself to infinite diversification. That is why *sunyata* is said to be a reservoir of infinite possibilities and not just a state of mere emptiness. Differentiating itself and yet remaining in itself undifferentiated, and thus to go on eternally engaged in the work of creation —this is *sunyata*, the *prajna*-continuum. It is not a concept reached by intellection, but what is given as pure act, as pure experience; it is a point fully charged with creative *élan vital*, which can transform itself into a straight line, into a plane, into a tridimensional body.

Now we can understand what is meant by this saying: Creation is contemplation and contemplation is creation. When *sunyata* remains in itself and with itself, it is contemplation; when it subjects itself to differentiation it creates. As this act of differentiation is not something imposed upon it but an act of self-generation, it is creation; we can say it is a creation out of nothing. *Sunyata* is not to be conceived statically but dynamically, or, better, as at once static and dynamic. The *prajna*-continuum thus creates through contemplation and contemplates through creation.

In *prajna*, therefore, there is an eternal progression and at the same time a never-changing state of unification.

Eternally evolving, endlessly limiting itself, *prajna* never loses its identity in *vijnana*. Logically speaking, *prajna*-creativity involves an interminable series of contradictions: *prajna* in *vijnana* and *vijnana* in *prajna* in every possible form and in every possible manner. There thus takes place a state of infinitely complicated interpenetration of *prajna* and *vijnana*. But we must not understand this spatially. For this most thoroughgoing interpenetration, indefinably complicated and yet subject to systematization, is the self-weaving net of *prajna*, and *vijnana* takes no active part in it. When, therefore, there is *prajna*-intuition, all this "mystery" yields its secrets, whereas, as long as our vision does not go beyond *vijnana*, we cannot penetrate to its very foundation and will naturally fail to perceive how *prajna* works into *vijnana*.

## NOTES

(1) *Prajna, pra-jna*, is the fundamental noetic principle whereby a synthetic apprehension of the whole becomes possible.

(2) *Vijnana, vi-jna-na*, is the principle of differentiation.

(3) *Dharma* is derived from the root "*dhr*", "to subsist", "to endure", and is used for a variety of meanings: "substance", "existence", "object", "teaching", "doctrine", "principle", "truth", "law", "relation", "norm", etc.

(4) *Atman* is "self", "the free-will", "one who is master of self". When Buddhist philosophy denies the existence of the self it means that there is no self-governing free-willing agent in the individual as long as it is a conditioned being, for the individual owes its birth to a combination of conditions which are always subject to dissolution, and anything liable to birth-and-death cannot be thought of as a free-willing, self-governing agent. A free-willing agent means a unifying principle.

(5) *Prajna-paramita* is one of the six perfections (*paramitas*): giving (*dana*), moral precepts (*sila*), humility (*ksanti*), diligence (*virya*), meditation (*dhyana*), and transcendental wisdom or absolute knowledge (*prajna*). "*Paramita*" is generally translated "going over to the other shore"—meaning that when these

items are practised one will finally cross the stream of birth-and-death. The *sutras* classified under the general title of *Prajnaparamita* expound the philosophy of *prajna*-intuition or *sunyata*.

(6) The *Diamond Sutra* is one of the "*Prajnaparamita*" *sutras* and contains the gist of *prajna* philosophy. Being short, it is very popularly read by Buddhists. There are several translations into English.

(7) The verse is by Zenne Daishi, popularly known as Fu Daishi (497–569), a contemporary of Bodhidharma. The verse in full runs thus:

> Empty-handed, I hold the spade;
> Walking, I ride on an ox;
> A man passes over the bridge;
> The bridge flows and the water does not.

(8) Masters of *prajna* philosophy make use of any object near their person to demonstrate the logic of *prajna*-intuition. The staff or *shippe* (a stick shorter than the staff) is frequently used for the purpose. Sometimes the question takes this form: "I do not call this a staff; what do you call it?"

(9) The idea of being quick is well illustrated by Tokusan (790–865), who displayed his staff lavishly and refused to listen to any talk. Once he announced that "you commit a fault when you ask a question; you also commit a fault when you do not ask". A monk came forward and bowed to him, preparing to say something. Tokusan struck him. The monk protested: "I have just been bowing to you, and why do you strike me?" The master said: "If I wait for you to open your mouth, nothing avails!" *Records of the Transmission of the Lamp* (Tokyo: Kokyoshoin 1881), xv, 122a. This edition is used throughout this paper. Hereafter, *R.T.L.*

(10) Ummon (?–949) once raised his staff forward and said: "When you see the staff call it a staff; when you see the post call it a post; and what fault could there be?" At another time he said: "What do you call this? If you say it is a staff, you go to hell; if not, what is it?" At still another time he brought the staff forward and said: "Common people would call this a reality; the Hinayana Buddhists would analyse it and declare that it is non-existent; the *pratyekabuddhas* would call it a visionary existence; the *bodhisattvas* would say that the staff is *sunya* (empty), as it is. As for Zen monks, they just call

the staff a staff; if they want to walk, they walk, if they want to sit they sit; no wavering in any circumstances!" *Sayings of Ummon* (Gotoyegen 1861), fasc. xv, pp. 1–7.

(11) *R.T.L.*, xxi, 38b.   (12) *R.T.L.*, xix, 23a; *Sayings of Ummon.*   (13) *R.T.L.*, xix, 22b.   (14) *R.T.L.*, xix, 23a. (15) *R.T.L.*, v, 80.   (16) *R.T.L.*, xix, 25a.   (17) *Hekigan-shu* (Ning-po 1876), case xix.

(18) *R.T.L.*, xi, 86b. Isan sent a mirror to his disciple Kyozan. Kyozan, producing it before the congregation, said: "Is this Isan's mirror or is it Kyozan's? If you can say a word about it, I will not break it." The whole Brotherhood did not say a word, and Kyozan smashed it.

(19) *Sayings of Rinzai* (Kyoto 1648). Once when Fuke and Rinzai were invited out to dinner, Rinzai remarked: "A hair swallows the great ocean and the seed of a poppy holds Mt. Sumeru in it: What does this mean?" Fuke, without saying a word, upset the whole table. The following day they were again invited out. Rinzai said: "How much is today's dinner like yesterday's?" Fuke again upset the table. Rinzai said: "What a rude fellow you are!" Fuke retorted at once: "In Buddhism there is neither rudeness nor politeness. What a blind fellow you are!"

(20) Tokusan, on his way to Taisan, felt hungry and tired and stopped at a roadside teahouse and asked for refreshments. The old woman who kept the house, finding that Tokusan was a great student of the *Diamond Sutra*, said: "I have a question to ask you; if you can answer it I will serve you refreshments for nothing, but if you fail you have to go somewhere else for them." As Tokusan agreed, the woman proposed this: "In the *Diamond Sutra* we read that 'The past mind is unattainable; the present mind is unattainable; the future mind is unattainable'; and so, with what mind do you wish to punctuate?" (Refreshments are known in Chinese as *ten-jin* (*t'ien-hsin*), meaning "punctuating the mind", hence the question.) Tokusan was altogether non-plussed, and did not know how to answer. He had to go without anything to eat. "The past mind" and so on require a somewhat detailed explanation which I omit here.

(21) *R.T.L.*, xxiv, 65b.   (22) *R.T.L.*, xxv, 78b. (23) *R.T.L.*, xxv, 73b.

(24) As in the case of "An inch's difference and heaven-and-earth's separation", the original Chinese for this quotation is also extremely terse and loses a great deal of its force

in translation. The original runs like this: "Sogen's one-drop-water." The question: "What is Sogen's one-drop-water?" The answer: "Sogen's one-drop-water." (Sogen means "Sokei source".)

(25) *R.T.L.*, xxv, under "Tokusho".    (26) This refers to the Absolute (*Sunyata*).

(27) Literally, "to turn things", or "to transform things".

(28) When a lion roars the *yakan's* head splits. The *yakan* is an insignificant creature.

(29) *R.T.L.*, xxv, 74b.    (30) *R.T.L.*, xxv, 78b.

(31) *Samadhi* means a state of intense concentration, in which the subject becomes identified with the object. This is often mistaken for *prajna*-intuition. So long as there is no *prajna* awakening, *samadhi* is merely a psychological phenomenon.

(32) *R.T.L.*, xxvi, 93a.    (33) *R.T.L.*, xxvi, 85b.    (34) Ibid. (35) Ibid.    (36) *R.T.L.*, xxiv, 114b.    (37) *R.T.L.*, xxv, 77b. (38) *R.T.L.*, xxvi, 86b.    (39) *R.T.L.*, xxii, 45b.    (40) *R.T.L.*, xx, 30a.    (41) *R.T.L.*, xxi, 41a.    (42) *R.T.L.*, xxi, 40a. (43) *R.T.L.*, xxi, 38a.    (44) *R.T.L.*, xxvi, 87b.    (45) *R.T.L.*, xxi, 38b.    (46) *R.T.L.*, xxi, 41b.    (47) *R.T.L.*, xix, 21a. (48) *R.T.L.*, xviii, 16b.    (49) *R.T.L.*, xxvi, 85b.    (50) Ibid. (51) Ibid.    (52) Ibid.    (53) *R.T.L.*, xxiv, 72a.    (54) *R.T.L.*, xxvi, 87b.

(55) "Revolving" refers to the reading of the *sutra*. When certain *sutras* are read they are simply unrolled and folded back, and this is repeated several times. The *sutras* being too long for a regular reading, the priests resort to this simplified method. Thus *sutra*-reading came to be known as "*sutra*-revolving", though in this case the actual *sutra*-revolving has nothing to do with the master's enigmatic statement.

(56) *R.T.L.*, xxvi, 86b.

(57) As is already well known to the reader, the masters frequently make such factually impossible statements. The idea is to make the questioners, that is, all objectively minded people, reverse their way of thinking. Ultimately, this means to re-examine our ordinary "logical" way of reasoning.

(58) *R.T.L.*, xxvi, 86b.    (59) *R.T.L.*, xxv, 78b. (60) *R.T.L.*, xxvi, 87b.    (61) *R.T.L.*, xxv, 78a.    (62) *R.T.L.*, xxiii, 55a.    (63) *R.T.L.*, xiv, 117b.

(64) *R.T.L.*, xiv, 115a. Tanka was a great master of Zen philosophy in the T'ang dynasty. One winter night when he was staying at a certain monastery, he felt very cold, and so he took down the wooden image of Buddha from the shrine

and burned it to make a fire. When he was blamed for this sacrilegious deed, he simply said that he just wanted to collect the *sarira* of the Buddha-image. When he was told that no *sarira* could be obtained from the wood, he said: "Why, then, do you blame me?" (The *sarira* is some mineral matter which is sometimes found in the ashes when the body is cremated. The holier the man, the more and brighter the *sarira*, it is said.) I may add an encounter Tanka had with the daughter of his friend Hokoji. Both Hokoji and his daughter were advanced in their understanding of Zen. When Tanka called one day on Hokoji, he met his daughter picking vegetables in the garden. Asked Tanka: "Is your father home?" The girl did not say anything in answer, but, throwing down the basket she carried, she stood up with her hands folded over her chest. Tanka asked again: "Is he home?" The girl took up the basket and walked away.

(65) In Buddhism food and other offerings, such as flowers, incense, and candles, are placed before the Buddha-image and other holy images as tokens of gratitude for what they have done.

(66) This refers to the story of an old Buddhist philosopher. He made the stones nod when he talked earnestly about the *dharma* to the stones, as he had no human audience. (*See* p. 195.)

# V. ZEN: A REPLY TO
# DR. HU SHIH

(Being Professor D. T. Suzuki's Reply to an Article by Dr. Hu Shih, sometime President of the National Peking University, entitled "Ch'an (Zen) Buddhism in China, Its History and Method". The Reply was printed, together with Dr. Hu Shih's article, in *Philosophy East and West*, for April 1953 (Vol. III, No. 1), published by the University of Hawaii Press. Both the summary of the Article and Dr. Suzuki's Reply are reprinted here by kind permission of the Editor of *Philosophy East and West*, Dr. Charles A. Moore.)

## EDITORIAL NOTE

A REPLY to an Article is seldom of value unless accompanied by the article to which it is the Reply. In this case, however, Dr. Suzuki's observations on Dr. Hu Shih's account of the history of Zen Buddhism in China is all but complete in itself, as a treatise on the futility of seeking to pin Zen to this or any other period of history. A few extracts from Dr. Hu Shih's article, together with a summary of passages to which Dr. Suzuki refers, will therefore suffice as an introduction to the text of the Reply.

Dr. Hu Shih's article begins as follows:

"Is Ch'an (Zen) beyond our Understanding?

"For more than a quarter of a century, my learned friend, Dr. Daisetz Teitaro Suzuki, formerly of the Otani University, Kyoto, Japan, has been interpreting and introducing Zen Buddhism to the Western world. Through his untiring effort and through his many books on Zen, he has succeeded in winning an audience and a number of followers, notably in England.

"As a friend and as a historian of Chinese thought, I have followed Suzuki's work with keen interest. But I have never concealed from him my disappointment in his method of approach. My greatest disappointment has been that, according to Suzuki and his disciples, Zen is illogical, irrational, and, therefore, beyond our intellectual understanding. In his book *Living by Zen* Suzuki tells us:

> " 'If we are to judge Zen from our common-sense view of things, we shall find the ground sinking away under our feet. Our so-called rationalistic way of thinking has apparently no use in evaluating the truth or untruth of Zen. It is altogether beyond the ken of human understanding. All that we can therefore state about Zen is that its uniqueness lies in its irrationality or its passing beyond our logical comprehension.'

"It is this denial of the capability of the human intelligence to understand and evaluate Zen that I emphatically refuse to accept. Is the so-called Ch'an or Zen really so illogical and irrational that it is 'altogether beyond the ken of human understanding' and that our rational or rationalistic way of thinking is of no use 'in evaluating the truth and untruth of Zen'?

"The Ch'an (Zen) movement is an integral part of the history of Chinese Buddhism, and the history of Chinese Buddhism is an integral part of the general history of Chinese thought. Ch'an can be properly understood only in its historical setting just as any other Chinese philosophical school must be studied and understood in its historical setting.

"The main trouble with the 'irrational' interpreters of Zen has been that they deliberately ignore this historical approach. 'Zen,' says Suzuki, 'is above space-time relations, and naturally even above historical facts.' Any man who takes this unhistorical and anti-historical position can never understand the Zen movement or the teaching of the great Zen masters. Nor can he hope to make Zen properly understood by the people of the East or the West. The best he can do is to tell the world that

Zen is Zen and is altogether beyond our logical comprehension.

"But if we restore the Zen movement to its 'space-time relations', that is, place it in its proper historical setting, and study it and its seemingly strange teachings as 'historical facts', then, but not until then, an intelligent and rational understanding and appreciation of this great movement in Chinese intellectual and religious history may yet be achieved."

Then follows a brief history of Zen Buddhism in China, beginning in the eighth century with the challenge of Shen-hui to the claim that Shen-hsiu and not Hui-neng was the Sixth Patriarch of Zen after Bodhidharma. Shen-hui proclaimed that the doctrine of Sudden Enlightenment was the sole true teaching of the Buddha and of all who succeeded him, and this in the face of the Gradual Englightenment proclaimed by Shen-hsiu. As the result of Shen-hui's tremendous and sustained efforts Hui-neng was in due course officially recognized as the Sixth Patriarch in the place of Shen-hsiu. Dr. Hu-Shih then gives a description of the seven schools of Ch'an in the eighth century, and of the great persecution of Buddhism of the ninth century.

Then follows the final section on "The Development of the Method of Ch'an" which is the passage in the article about which Dr. Suzuki has most to say.

"The age of Ch'an as an epoch in the history of Chinese thought covered about four hundred years—from about A.D. 700 to 1100. The first century and a half was the era of the great founders of Chinese Ch'an, —the era of dangerous thinking, courageous doubting and plain speaking. All authentic documents of that period show that the great masters, from Shen-hui and Ma-tsu to Hsuan-chien and I-hsuan, taught and spoke in plain and unmistakable language and did not resort to enigmatic words, gestures, or acts. Some of the famous enigmatic answers attributed to Ma-tsu and his immediate disciples were undoubtedly very late inventions.

"But as the Ch'an schools became respectable and even fashionable in intellectual and political circles, there arose monks and lay dilettantes who talked and prattled in the language of the Ch'an masters without real understanding and without conviction. There was real danger that the great ideas of the founders of the Ch'an schools were deteriorating into what has been called 'ch'an of the mouth-corners' (k'ou-t'ou ch'an). Moreover, Ch'an was rapidly replacing all other forms of Buddhism, and prominent Ch'an masters of the mountains were often called to head large city monasteries. They had to perform or officiate at many Buddhist rituals of worship demanded by the public or the State even though they might sincerely believe that there were no Buddhas or *bodhisattvas*. Were they free to tell their powerful patrons, on whom the institution had to rely for support, that 'the Buddha was a murderer who had seduced many people into the pitfalls of the Devil'? Could there be some other subtle but equally thought-provoking way of expressing what the earlier masters had said outspokenly?

"All these new situations, and probably many others, led to the development of a pedagogical method of conveying a truth through a great variety of strange and sometimes seemingly crazy gestures, words, or acts. I-hsuan himself was probably the first to introduce these techniques, for he was famous for beating his questioner with a stick or shouting a deafening shout at him. It was probably no accident that his school, the Lin-chi school, played a most prominent part during the next hundred years in the development of the peculiar methodology of Ch'an instruction to take the place of plain speaking.

"But this methodology with all its mad techniques is not so illogical and irrational as it has often been described. A careful and sympathetic examination of the comparatively authentic records of the Ch'an schools and of the testimony of contemporary witnesses and critics has convinced me that beneath all the apparent madness and confusion there is a conscious and rational method which may be described as a method of education by the hard way, by letting the individual find out things through his own effort and through his own ever-widening life-experience.

"Broadly speaking, there are three stages or phases in this pedagogical method.

"First, there is the basic principle which was stated as *pu shuo p'o*, 'never tell too plainly'. It is the duty of the teacher never to make things too easy for the novice; he must not explain things in too plain language; he must encourage him to do his own thinking and to find out things for himself. Fa-yen (died 1104), one of the greatest teachers of Ch'an, used to recite these lines of unknown authorship:

You may examine and admire the embroidered drake.
But the golden needle which made it, I'll not pass on to you.

"This is so important that Chu Hsi (1130–1200), the greatest Confucianist thinker and teacher of the twelfth century, once said to his students: 'The school of Confucius and that of Lao-tzu and Chuang-tzu left no great successors to carry on the work of the founders. But the Ch'an Buddhists can always find their own successors, and that is due to the fact that they are prepared to run the risk of explaining nothing in plain language, so that others may be left to do their own pondering and puzzling, out of which a real threshing-out may result.' One of the great Ch'an masters often said: 'I owe everything to my teacher because he never explained anything plainly to me.'

"Secondly, in order to carry out the principle of 'never tell too plainly', the Ch'an teachers of the ninth and tenth centuries devised a great variety of eccentric methods of answering questions. If a novice should ask some such question as 'What is truth?' or 'What is Buddhism?' the master would almost surely box him on the ear, or give him a beating with a cane, or retire into a stern silence. Some less rude teacher would tell the questioner to go back to the kitchen and wash the dishes. Others would answer questions with seemingly meaningless or strikingly meaningful paradoxes.

"Thus, when the master Wen-yen (died 949), founder of the Yün-men School, was asked 'What is the Buddha like?' he answered: 'A dried stick of dung.' (This is so profanely iconoclastic that Suzuki probably deliberately mistranslates it as 'A dried-up dirt-cleaner', which, of course, is incorrect and meaningless.) Such an answer is not nonsensical at all; it harks back to the iconoclastic teachings of his spiritual grandfather, Hsuan-chien, who had actually said: 'The Buddha is a dried piece of dung of the barbarians, and sainthood is only an empty name.'

"Thus Liang-chia (died 869), one of the founders of the Ts-aoshan-Tungshan School, when asked the same question, said quietly: 'Three *chin* (about three pounds) of hemp,' which, too, is not meaningless if one remembers the naturalistic thinking of some of the masters of the earlier era.

"But the novice in all probability would not understand. So, he retires to the kitchen and washes the dishes. He is puzzled and feels ashamed of his failure to understand. After some time, he is told to leave the place and try his luck elsewhere. Here he begins the *third stage* of his education—the third and most important phase of the pedagogical method, which was called *hsing-chiao*, 'travelling on foot'."

Travelling on foot, carrying only a stick, a bowl, and a pair of sandals, and begging for food and lodging, toughened the pilgrim's physical and mental fibres, says Dr. Hu Shih. It enabled him to see the world and to meet all kinds of people, including the great minds of the age, and this in time brought him to the point where a trifling incident would bring him to Sudden Enlightenment. Dr. Hu Shih concludes:

"Was this Ch'an illogical and irrational and beyond our intellectual understanding?" He replies to himself in the story told by Fa-yen, the Ch'an master of the eleventh century, about the expert burglar and the way in which he taught his son his trade. Readers will find it in Nuka-

riya's *The Religion of the Samurai* at pp. 179–80, and in
Dr. Suzuki's First Series of *Essays in Zen Buddhism* at pp.
296–7 of the first edition and pp. 310–11 of the second.

## DR. SUZUKI'S REPLY

One of my first impressions after reading Dr. Hu Shih's
learned and instructive paper on Zen Buddhism in China
is that he may know a great deal about history but
nothing about the actor behind it. History is a kind of
public property accessible to everybody who is at liberty
to handle it according to his judgment. To this extent
history is something objective, and its materials or facts,
though these are quite an indefinite element in the
make-up of history, are like scientific objects ready to be
examined by the students. They are not, of course, subject
to planned experiments. On the other hand, the actor or
creator, the man who is behind history, eludes the
historian's objective handling. What constitutes his
individuality or subjectivity cannot be made the object
of historical investigation, because it refuses to manifest
itself objectively. It can be appreciated only by himself.
His is a unique existence which can never be duplicated,
and this uniqueness in its metaphysical sense, or in its
deepest sense, can be intuited only by the man himself.
It is not the historian's business to peer into it. In fact,
however much he may try, he will always be frustrated
in his attempt. Hu Shih fails to understand this.

A further impression is that, vis-à-vis Zen, there are
at least two types of mentality; the one which can understand Zen and, therefore, has the right to say something
about it, and another which is utterly unable to grasp what
Zen is. The difference between the two types is one of
quality and is beyond the possibility of reconciliation.
By this I mean that, from the point of view of the second
type, Zen belongs in a realm altogether transcending
this type of mind and, therefore, is not a worthwhile
subject on which to waste much time. Men of the

first type know very well where this second type is entrenched, because they were there themselves prior to their attainment to Zen.

It is my opinion that Hu Shih, who represents the second type of mentality, is not properly qualified to discuss Zen as Zen apart from its various historical settings. Zen must be understood from the inside, not from the outside. One must first attain what I call *prajna*-intuition and then proceed to the study of all its objectified expressions. To try to get into Zen by collecting the so-called historical materials and to come to a conclusion which will definitely characterize Zen as Zen, Zen in itself, or Zen as each of us lives it in his innermost being, is not the right approach.

Hu Shih, as a historian, knows Zen in its historical setting, but not Zen in itself. It is likely that he does not recognize that Zen has its own life independent of history. After he has exhausted Zen in its historical setting, he is not aware of the fact that Zen is still fully alive, demanding Hu Shih's attention and, if possible, his "unhistorical" treatment.

2

Hu Shih seems upset by my statement that Zen is irrational and beyond our intellectual comprehension, and he tries to show that Zen can be understood easily when it is placed in its historical setting. He thinks that when Zen is so placed, it is found that the Zen movement in the history of Chinese Buddhism was "only a part of a larger movement which may be correctly characterized as internal reformation or revolution in Buddhism". Let me see if he is right.

My contention is twofold: (1) Zen is not explainable by mere intellectual analysis. As long as the intellect is concerned with words and ideas, it can never reach Zen. (2) Even when Zen is treated historically, Hu Shih's way of setting it in a historical frame is not correct, because he fails to understand what Zen is. I must strongly insist that Zen must first be comprehended as it is in itself; only then can one proceed to the study of its historical objectifications, as Hu Shih does.

I will discuss the second point first.

Hu Shih does not seem to understand the real significance of "sudden awakening or enlightenment" in its historical setting. He makes a great deal of Tao-sheng's allusion to this term and thinks that here is the beginning of Zen thought. But "sudden enlightenment" is the very essence of Buddhist teaching, and all the schools of Buddhism, Hinayana and Mahayana, Yoga-cara and Madhyamika, even, in my opinion, the Pure Land sect, owe their origin to Buddha's enlightenment-experience which he had under the Bodhi tree by the River Nairanjana so many centuries ago. Buddha's enlightenment was no other than a "sudden enlightenment". Among the *sutras* in which this experience is emphasized, I may mention the *Vimalakirti*, the *Lanka-vatara*, and the *Sutra of Perfect Enlightenment*. Though the last-mentioned is a disputed *sutra*, it is one of the most important works on Zen.

In the history of Zen, Yeno (Hui-neng or Wei-lang in Chinese) comes foremost, and it may be better in more than one sense to consider him the first Patriarch of Zen in China. His message was really revolutionary. Though he is described as an illiterate son of a farmer, living in the Lingnan district far away from the centre of T'ang culture and civilization, he was a great pioneer spirit and opened up a new field in the study of Buddhism, upsetting all the traditions which preceded him. His message was: *dhyana* and *prajna* are one; where *dhyana* is, there is *prajna*, and where *prajna* is, there is *dhyana;* they are not to be separated one from the other.[1] Before Hui-neng the two were regarded as separate; at least their identity was not clearly affirmed, which resulted in the practice of emphasizing *dhyana* at the expense of *prajna*. Buddha's all-important enlightenment-experience

[1] Cf. *The Dhammahada*, verse 372.

came to be interpreted statically and not dynamically, and the doctrine of *sunyata* (emptiness), which is really the cornerstone of Buddhist thought-structure, became a dead thing. Hui-neng revived the enlightenment-experience.

According to *The Records of the Lanka Teachers and Disciples*, Tao-hsin (Doshin), popularly known as the fourth Patriarch of Zen in China, was a great master of Zen, and under his successor, Hung-jen (Gunin), the fifth Patriarch, there were ten or eleven great masters, one of whom was Hui-neng (Yeno). Tao-hsin and Hung-jen, however, did not make the distinction and the identity of *dhyana* and *prajna* quite clear. Perhaps there were yet no impelling circumstances to do so. But under Hung-jen this changed, for among the rivals of Hui-neng there was Shen-hsiu (Jinshu), who was an outstanding figure almost overshadowing Hui-neng. Shen-hsiu was a contrast to Hui-neng in every way— in learning, monkish training, and personality. Hui-neng stayed in the South, while Shen-hsiu went to the capital under imperial patronage. It was natural that Shen-hsiu and his teaching were more esteemed. Hui-neng, however, did not make any special effort to compete with Shen-hsiu, doing his own preaching in his own way in the remote provincial towns. It was due to Shen-hui, one of the youngest disciples of Hui-neng, that the differences between Hui-neng's school and Shen-hsiu's were brought to the surface and the great struggle started for ascendance and supremacy, as described so well by Hu Shih.

Shen-hui's emphasis, however, on the doctrine of sudden enlightenment does not exactly reflect the true spirit of Hui-neng. It is rather a side-issue from the doctrine of the identity of *dhyana* and *prajna*. According to my "historical understanding", the identity-doctrine comes first and when this is grasped sudden enlightenment naturally follows. Shen-hui probably had to emphasize sudden enlightenment because of strong opposition from Shen-hsiu's followers. Shen-hui's position is better understood from Tsung-mi's comment on Shen-hui in which Tsung-mi characterizes Shen-hui's teaching as "The one character *chih* is the gateway to all secrets". Here *chih* means *prajna*-intuition and not "knowledge" in its ordinary sense. When *chih* is rendered—as it is by Hu Shih—as "knowledge", all is lost, not only Shen-hui and Hui-neng but also Zen itself. *Chih* here is the key-term which unlocks all the secrets of Zen. I will return to this later.

That *dhyana* is no other than *prajna* was Hui-neng's intuition, which was really revolutionary in the history of Buddhist thought in China. Chih-i was a great Buddhist philosopher, and Fa-tsang was a still greater one. The latter marks the climax of Buddhist thought as it developed in China. Fa-tsang's systematization of ideas expounded in the Buddhist *sutra*-group known as the *Gandavyuha* or *Avatamsaka* (Kegon in Japanese and Hua-yen in Chinese) is one of the wonderful intellectual achievements performed by the Chinese mind and is of the highest importance to the history of world thought. Hui-neng's accomplishment in the way of Zen intuition equals, indeed, in its cultural value that of Chih-i and Fa-tsang, both of whom are minds of the highest order, not only in China but in the whole world.

What, then, is the identity-doctrine of Hui-neng? How did it contribute to the later development of the various schools of Zen Buddhism? To answer these is more than I can manage in this paper.[1] Let me just refer to Shen-hui. While Shen-hui was engaged in discussion with Ch'eng, the Zen master, on the subject of identity, Shen-hui remarked to Wang Wei, who was the host: "When I am thus talking with you I am the identity of *dhyana* and *prajna*."[2] This gives the doctrine in a nutshell, or it may be better to say that Shen-hui himself stands here as the practical demonstrator of it. From this identity naturally follows Ma-tsu's famous dictum:

---

[1] I have treated these problems in the third volume of my "History of Zen Thought". The book is in Japanese and is still in MS.

[2] Suzuki's edition of *Shen-Hui-Sayings* [or *Discourses*], pp. 31–2.

"My everyday thought is the *Tao*" (*heijo-shin kore michi*; in Chinese, *p'ing ch'ang hsin shih tao*). This is explained by him thus: "Everyday thought means to be doing nothing special; it means to be free from right and wrong, to be free from taking and giving up, to be free from nihilism as well as eternalism, to be neither a saintly nor an ordinary man, neither a wise man nor a *bodhisattva*. My going-about, standing, sitting, or lying-down; my meeting situations as they arise; my dealing with things as they come and go—all this is the *Tao*."[1]

To give a few more examples of the identity-doctrine as it developed later:

A monk asked Kei-shin of Chosha (Changsha Ching-ts'en), who was a disciple of Nansen Fugwan (Nanch'uan Pu-yuan, died 834): "What is meant by 'everyday thought'?" Kei-shin answered: "If you want to sleep, sleep; if you want to sit, sit." The monk said: "I do not understand." Kei-shin answered: "When hot, we try to get cool; when cold, we turn toward a fire."

A monk asked Kei-shin: "According to Nansen, the cat and the ox have a better knowledge of it than all the Buddhas of the past, the present, and the future. How is it that all the Buddhas do not know it?"

Kei-shin answered: "They knew a little better before they entered the Deer Park."

The monk: "How is it that the cat and ox have a knowledge of it?"

Kei-shin: "You cannot suspect them."[2]

This *mondo* will be understood better when I try later to distinguish two kinds of knowledge, relative and transcendental. Hu Shih may think this is a "crazy" kind of Zen methodology to make the monk realize the truth by himself in a most straightforward way.

In one sense, this way of looking at life may be judged to be a kind of naturalism, even of animalistic libertinism.

[1] Tao Yuan, *Ching Te Ch'uan Teng Lu* (*The Record of the Transmission of the Lamp*), Fas. XXVIII.
[2] Ibid, Fas. X.

But we must remember that man is human, and the animal is animal. There must be a distinction between human naturalism and animal naturalism. We ask questions and wait and decide and act, but animals do not ask questions, they just act. This is where they have one advantage over us, and yet this is where they are animals. Human naturalism is not quite the same as animal naturalism. We are hungry. Sometimes we decide not to eat; sometimes we even decide to starve to death, and here is human naturalism, too. It may be called unnaturalism.

There is, however, through all these naturalistic affirmations or unnaturalistic negations, something that is in every one of us which leads to what I call a transcendental "yes" attitude or frame of mind. This can be seen in the Zen master when he asserts: "Just so", or "So it is", or "You are right", or "Thus things go", or "Such is the way", etc. In the Chinese the assertion runs: *shih mo*, or *chih mo*, or *ju shih*, or *ju tz'u*, or *chih che shih*. These do not exhaust all the statements a Zen master makes in the expression of his "yes" frame of mind, or in his acceptance of the Buddhist doctrine of suchness or thusness (*tathata*) or of emptiness (*sunyata*).[1]

Strictly speaking, there cannot be a philosophy of suchness, because suchness defies a clear-cut definition as an idea. When it is presented as an idea it is lost; it turns into a shadow, and any philosophy built on it will be a castle on the sand. Suchness or *chih che shih* is something one has to experience in oneself. Therefore, we might say that it is only by those who have this experience that any provisional system of thought can be produced on the basis of it. In many cases such minds prefer silence to

[1] As regards the idea of "suchness" (*sono mama* in Japanese, *shih mo* in Chinese, and *tathata* in Sanskrit), which I hold to be the basis of all religious experience, the reader is referred to Exodus iv, 14, where God reveals his name to Moses as "I am that I am"; and also to Jacques Maritain's *A Preface to Metaphysics*, p. 93, where he expounds "the principle of identity" as "being is being". My article on "Japanese Thought", which is my contribution to *History of Philosophy Eastern and Western* (Allen and Unwin, 1952), Vol. I, pp. 597 ff., will also shed light on the idea of *sono mama* or *kannagara* in Shinto terminology.

verbalism or what we may call symbolism to intellectualization. They do not like to risk any form of misunderstanding, for they know that the finger is quite liable to be taken for the moon. The Zen master, generally speaking, despises those who indulge in word- or idea-mongering, and in this respect Hu Shih and myself are great sinners, murderers of Buddhas and patriarchs; we are both destined for hell.

But it is not a bad thing to go to hell, if it does some good to somebody. So, let us go on our way and I, for my part, quote the following from *The Transmission of the Lamp* (Fas. XIV) under Yakusan Igen (Yaoshan Wei-yen, 751–834), and hope to help readers understand what I mean by the experience of suchness, or the *chih che shih* frame of mind:

One day Yakusan was found quietly sitting in meditation. Sekito (Shih-t'ou, 700–790), seeing this, asked: "What are you doing here?"
Yakusan answered: "I am not doing anything at all."
Sekito said: "In that case you are just sitting idly."
Yakusan: "If I am sitting idly, I am then doing something."
Sekito: "You say you are not doing anything. What is this 'anything' you are not doing?"
Yakusan: "You may get a thousand wise men together and even they cannot tell."
Sekito then composed a stanza:

Since of old we have been living together without
    knowing the name;
Hand in hand, as the wheel turns, we thus go.[1]

[1] "Thus" in the original Chinese is *chih mo* (*shimo* in Japanese). This term coupled with *jen-yun* is the essence of this *gatha*. "*Jen-yun*", here translated "as the wheel turns" or "as the wind blows", has nothing to do with fatalism. "*Jen-yun*" frequently goes with "*t'eng-t'eng*" (sometimes *teng-teng*). This combination "*jen-yun t'eng-t'eng*" is full of significance, but it is very difficult to give the idea in a few English words. In short, it is "Let thy will be done" without the accompaniment of "My God, my God, why hast thou forsaken me?" "*T'eng-t'eng*" is going around almost jubilantly, at least in a fully relaxed state of mind, with no fear, no anxiety, no anguish.

Since ancient times even wise men of the highest grade
failed to know what it is;
How then can ordinary people expect to have a clear
understanding of it in a casual way?

Sometime later, Sekito remarked: "Words and actions are
of no avail."

To this Yakusan said: "Even when there are no words, no
actions, they are of no avail."

Sekito said: "Here is no room even for a pinhead."

Yakusan then said: "Here it is like planting a flower on
the rock."

And Sekito expressed his full approval.

When Beirei Osho (Mi-ling, the teacher)[1] was about to
pass away, he left this in part for his disciples: "O my pupils,
carefully think of the matter. Ultimately, it is 'just this and
nothing more,' *chih che shih*!"

A monk asked Risan Osho[2] (Li-shan, the teacher):
"What is the idea of Daruma (*Tamo*) coming from the West?"

Risan answered: "I do not see any 'What'."

The monk: "Why so?"

Risan said: "Just so and nothing more" (*chih wei ju tz'u*).

*Chih ju tz'u, shih mo,* and *chih che shih*—all these are the
Zen masters' attempts to express what goes beyond
words or what cannot be mediated by ideas. When they
wish to be more expressive, they say: "It is like planting
a flower on the rock", or "A silly old man is filling the
well with snow", or "It is like piling vegetables into a
bottomless basket". The more they try to express themselves, the more enigmatic they become. They are not
doing this with any special pedagogic purpose. They
are just trying to give expression to what they have in
mind. Nor are they exponents of agnosticism. They are
just plain Zen masters who have something to say to
the rest of their fellow-beings.

Into whatever historical setting Zen may fit, and in
whatever way the historian may deal with it, as revolutionary or iconoclastic or anti-traditional, we must remember

[1] *The Transmission of the Lamp*, Fas. VIII, under "Beirei".
[2] Ibid., under "Risan".

that this kind of treatment of Zen never does clarify
the self-nature (*svabhava* or *svalaksana*) of Zen. The
historical handling of Zen cannot go any further than
the objective relationships with other so-called historical
factors. When this is done, however skilfully and in-
geniously, the historian cannot expect to have done with
Zen in every possible way. The fact is that if one is to
understand *what* Zen is *in itself* it has to be grasped from
within. Unfortunately, Hu Shih seems to neglect this
side of the study of Zen.

### 3

This neglect on the part of Hu Shih is shown in his
dealing with Tsung-mi's characterization of Shen-hui.
Tsung-mi (Shu-mitsu) sums up Shen-hui's teaching as
being centred in one Chinese character "*chih*", which is
regarded as "the gateway to all mysteries (or secrets)".
Hu Shih translates *chih* as "knowledge" and takes it as
best characterizing Shen-hui's intellectualistic approach.
This statement proves that Hu Shih does not understand Zen as it is in itself, apart from its "historical
setting".

Shen-hui's *chih* does not mean intellectual knowledge,
but is rather what I have called "*prajna*-intuition".[1]
It may take many pages to explain my position in regard
to *chih*, but I have to do it because it is the central notion
of Zen. And when one knows what *chih* is, one knows
something of Zen.

When Buddhist philosophers talk much about suchness or thusness, and when the Zen master raises his
eyebrows, or swings his stick, or coughs, or rubs his hands,
or utters the "*Ho!*" cry (*kwatz* in Japanese), or just says
"Yes, yes", or "You are right", or "Thus we go", almost

[1] See my paper on this in *Essays in East-West Philosophy: An Attempt at
World Philosophical Synthesis*, Charles A Moore, ed. (Honolulu: University
of Hawaii Press 1951), pp. 17–48.
[This is the preceding article in this Volume.—Ed.]

*ad infinitum*, we must remember that they all point to something in us which may be called pure self-consciousness, or pure experience, or pure awakening, or intuition (rather, *prajna*-intuition). This is the very foundation of all our experiences, all our knowledge, and defies being defined, for definition means ideation and objectification. The "something" is the ultimate reality or "*subjectum*" or "emptiness" (*sunyata*). And what is most important here is that it is self-conscious, though not in the relative sense. This self-consciousness is *chih*, and Tsung-mi and Shen-hui quite rightly make it the gateway to all Zen secrets.

I should like to have Hu Shih remember that knowledge, as the term is generally used, is the relationship between subject and object. Where there is no such dichotomous distinction, knowledge is impossible. If we have something of noetic quality here, we must not designate it as knowledge, for by doing so we get into confusion and find ourselves involved in contradictions. When the self becomes conscious of itself at the end of an ever-receding process of consciousness, this last is what we must call self-consciousness in its deepest sense. This is truly the consciousness of the self, where there is no subject-object separation, but where subject is object and object is subject. If we still find here the bifurcation of subject and object, that will not yet be the limit of consciousness. We have now gone beyond that limit and are conscious of this fact of transcendence. Here can be no trace of selfhood, only unconscious consciousness of no-self, because we are now beyond the realm of the subject-object relationship.

Shen-hui calls this *chih*, which is no other than *prajna*-intuition, or simply *prajna* in contradistinction to *vijnana*, "discriminatory knowledge". Here is the irrationality of Zen beyond the comprehension of human understanding. *Chih* is the absolute object of *prajna* and at the same time is *prajna* itself. The Chinese Buddhist philosophers frequently call it, tautologically, *pan-ju chih chih-hui* (*hannya no chiye* in Japanese), for they want to have *chih-hui*, as it is ordinarily understood, sharply distinguished from *prajna* (*pan-ju*).

The professional philosopher or historian may reject the existence and reality of *chih* as we have it here, because he, especially the historian, finds it rather disturbing in his objective and "historical" treatment of Zen. The historian here resorts to strange tactics. He summarily puts aside as "fabrication" or fiction or invention everything that does not conveniently fit into his scheme of historical setting. I would not call this kind of history objective but strongly coloured with subjectivism.

I am now ready to present a piece of Zen epistemology. There are two kinds of information we can have of reality; one is knowledge *about* it and the other is that which comes out of reality itself. Using "knowledge" in its broadest sense, the first is what I would describe as knowable knowledge and the second as unknowable knowledge.

Knowledge is knowable when it is the relationship between subject and object. Here are the subject as knower and the object as the known. As long as this dichotomy holds, all knowledge based on it is knowable because it is public property and accessible to everybody. On the contrary, knowledge becomes unknown or unknowable when it is not public but strictly private in the sense that it is not sharable by others.[1] Unknown knowledge is the result of an inner experience; therefore, it is wholly individual and subjective. But the strange thing about this kind of knowledge is that the one who has it is absolutely convinced of its universality in spite of its privacy. He knows that everybody has it, but everybody is not conscious of it.

Knowable knowledge is relative, while unknown knowledge is absolute and transcendental and is not communicable through the medium of ideas. Absolute

[1] In order to avoid any possible misunderstanding on the part of the reader, I add this: The experience is altogether private inasmuch as it is a form of feeling, but at the same time there is in it an element of universality. It is at once unsharable and sharable. It has in itself no paradox, but as soon as it expresses itself we encounter a paradox.

knowledge is the knowledge which the subject has of himself directly without any medium between him and his knowledge. He does not divide himself into factors such as subject and object in order to know himself. We may say that it is a state of inner awareness. And this awareness is singularly contributive to keeping one's mind free of fears and anxieties.

Unknown knowledge is intuitive knowledge. We must remember, however, that *prajna*-intuition is altogether different from perceptual intuitions. In the latter case there is the seer and the object which he sees, and they are separable and separate, one standing over against the other. They belong to the realm of relativity and discrimination. *Prajna*-intuition obtains where there is oneness and sameness. It is also different from ethical intuitions and from mathematical intuitions.

For a general characterization of *prajna*-intuition we can state something like this: *Prajna*-intuition is not derivative but primitive; not inferential, not rationalistic, nor mediational, but direct, immediate; not analytical but integrating; not cognitive, nor symbolical; not intending but merely expressive; not abstract, but concrete; not processional, not purposive, but factual and ultimate, final and irreducible; not eternally receding, but infinitely inclusive; etc. If we go on like this, there may be many more predicates which could be ascribed to *prajna*-intuition as its characteristics. But there is one quality we must not forget to mention in this connection; the uniqueness of *prajna*-intuition consists in its authoritativeness, utterly convincing and contributive to the feeling that "I am the ultimate reality itself", that "I am absolute knower", that "I am free and know no fear of any kind".[1] In one sense *prajna*-intuition may be said to correspond to Spinoza's *scientia intuitiva*. According to him, this kind of intuition is absolutely certain and infallible and, in contrast to *ratio*, produces the highest peace and virtue of the mind.

Let us see how these characterizations of *prajna*-

[1] Cf. *Dhammapada*, 153–4, 179.

intuition, which is no other than the Zen-experience,
fit the masters' way of handling Zen questions. I will
give just a few examples, enough to illustrate my point.

Dogo[1] asked Sekito:[2] "What is the ultimate Buddhist
teaching?"
Sekito answered: "Unless you have it you cannot tell."
Dogo: "Is there anything further which may give me a
clue?"
Sekito: "The vastness of the sky does not hinder the white
cloud flying anywhere it likes."

Another time, Dogo asked: "Who has attained the teaching
of the Sixth Patriarch?"
Sekito: "One who has understood Buddhism has it."
Dogo: "Do you have it?"
Sekito: "No, I do not understand Buddhism."

Superficially, this *mondo* ("question and answer") may
sound strange, because Sekito was actually under Yeno
(Hui-neng), the sixth Patriarch, when he was still very
young, and later came to understand Zen under one of
Hui-neng's principal disciples, Seigen Gyoshi.[3] What
makes him say, then, that he does not understand Hui-
neng's teaching—that is, Zen? In the first *mondo* Sekito
declares that unless one really understands what Buddhism
is one cannot tell what it is, which is quite a natural
thing to say. What, then, does he mean when he says that
he does not know Hui-neng's teaching? His knowledge
is evidently his not-knowing. This is "unknown knowledge".

A monk once asked Dai-ten (Ta-tien): "When the inside
men see each other what happens?"
Dai-ten answered: "They are already outside."

[1] Tao-wu Yen-chih, 779–835, *The Transmission of the Lamp*, Fas. XIV,
under "Sekito".
[2] Shih-tou Hsi-ch'ien, 742–55, ibid., Fas. XIV.
[3] Ch'ing-yuan Hang-ssu, died 740, ibid., Fas. V.

Monk: "How about those who are right inside?"
Dai-ten: "They do not ask such questions."[1]

One can readily see that this kind of *chih* is not knowledge that is transmissible to others, that it is subjective in the sense that it grows within oneself and is exclusively the possession of this particular person. We may call it "inside knowledge". But as soon as we say it is inside, it gets outside and ceases to be itself. You can neither affirm nor negate it. It is above both, but can be either as you choose.

Therefore, Yakusan[2] announced: "I have a word (*i chu tzu*) of which I have never told anybody."
Dogo said: "You are already giving yourself up to it."
Later a monk asked Yakusan: "What is the one word you do not tell anybody?"
Yakusan replied: "It is beyond talking."
Dogo remarked again: "You are already talking."

Yakusan's *i chu tzu* is no other than *chih*, "unknown and unknowable". It is the ultimate reality, the Godhead, in which there are no distinctions whatever and to which, therefore, the intellect cannot give any predicate, this or that, good or bad, right or wrong. To talk about it is to negate it. When Yakusan begins to talk about it either negatively or positively, his *i chu tzu* is no longer present. Dogo is right, therefore, in accusing his master of contradicting himself. But we can also say that Dogo has to share the same accusation he is throwing against the other. As far as human intellect is concerned, we can never escape this contradiction. Yakusan fully realizes this, but he cannot help himself inasmuch as he is also a human individual. The following records we have of him in *The Transmission of the Lamp* (Fas. XIV) show clearly where he stands:

A monk once asked him: "I have yet no clear knowledge of my self and may I ask you to indicate the way to it?"

[1] *The Transmission of the Lamp*, Fas. XIV, under "Ta-tien".
[2] Yaoshan Wei-yen, 754–834, ibid., Fas. XIV, under "Dogo" (Tao-un).

Yakusan remained silent for a while and then said: "It is not difficult for me to give you a word (*i chu*) about it. But what is needed of you is to see it instantly as the word is uttered. Then you may have something of it. But when you are given up to reflection or intellection (*ssu liang*) to any degree I shall be committing a fault myself and shall be blamed for it. It is better, therefore, to keep one's mouth tightly closed and let no trouble come out that way."

His is an honest confession.

The *i chu tzu* is an inner experience and defies expression in words, for words are mere symbols and cannot be the thing in itself. But as words are a convenient medium we have invented for mutual communication, we are apt to take them for realities. Money represents a good which is of real value, but we are so used to money that we manipulate it as if it were the value itself. Words are like money. The Zen masters know that; hence their persistent and often violent opposition to words and to the intellect which deals exclusively in words. This is the reason they appeal to the stick, the *hossu* (*fu-tzu*), the "Ho!" and to various forms of gesture. Even these are far from being the ultimate itself; the masters have faced a very difficult task in trying to convey what they have within themselves. Strictly speaking, however, there is no conveying at all. It is the awakening of the same experience in others by means of words, gestures, and anything the master finds suitable at the moment. There are no prescribed methods; there is no methodology set down in formulas.

To get further acquainted with the nature of *chih*, or *prajna*-intuition, let me quote more from *The Transmission of the Lamp*, which is the mine of the *mondo* and other Zen materials necessary for understanding Zen as far as such records are concerned.

A monk came to Dogo Yenchi (Tao-wu Yen-chih, 779–835) and asked: "How is it that the *Bodhisattva* of No-miracles leaves no traceable footsteps?"[1]

[1] *The Transmission of the Lamp*. Fas. XIV.

"Leaving no footsteps" has a specific meaning in Zen. This is what is expected of a highly trained Zen master. We ordinary people leave all kinds of footmarks by which our inner life can be detected and assessed. And this inner life is always found to be tainted with selfishness and motives arising from it and also with intellectual calculations designed for their execution. To leave no traces thus means in Christian terms to be above creaturely mindedness. It is, metaphysically speaking, to transcend both affirmation and negation, to be moving in the realm of oneness and sameness, and, therefore, to be leading a life of purposelessness (*anabhogacarya*) or of unattainability (*anupalabdha*). This is one of the most important notions in the philosophy of Zen. To trace the tracelessness of the Zen master's life is to have an "unknown knowledge" of the ultimate reality. Now let us see what answer was given by Dogo Yenchi (Tao-wu Yen-chih). It was simply this:

"One who goes with him knows it." ("Him" means the "*Bodhisattva* of No-miracles".)
The monk asked: "Do you know, O master?"
Dogo said: "I do not know."
The monk wanted to know the reason for his ignorance. "Why do you not, master?"
The master gave up the case. "You do not understand what I mean."

Now Dogo is no agnostic. He knows everything. He knows the monk through and through. His no-knowledge (*pu-chih*) is not to be "approached intellectually". It is of the same category as his *pu shih* when he answered Goho's (Wu-feng's) question: "Do you know Yakusan, the old master?" Goho wanted to know the reason, asking: "Why do you not know him?" Dogo said: "I do not, I do not." His answer was quite emphatic, as we see from his repetition of negation. This is a most flagrant repudiation of the "historical" fact, because Dogo was one of the chief disciples of Yakusan. This was well known among his contemporaries. Therefore, Goho's asking was not an ordinary question which called for information regarding human relationship. Dogo knew this full well, hence his "I do not know" (*pu shih pu shih*).

If I go on like this there will really be no ending. Let me hope that one more illustration will sufficiently clarify my position in regard to the meaning of the term "*chih*" as it was used by Shen-hui and Tsung-mi and by Zen people generally.

Ungan Donjo (Yun-yen T'an-sheng, died 841), disciple of Yakusan and the teacher of Tozan Ryokai,[1] once made this remark to the congregation: "There is a man for whom there is nothing he cannot answer if he is asked."
Tozan questioned: "How large is his library?"
The master said: "Not a book in his house."
Tozan: "How could he be so learned?"
The master: "Not a wink he sleeps day and night."
Tozan: "May I ask him some special question?"
The master: "His answer will be no answer."[2]

When the gist of these Zen *mondo* is replaced more or less by modern phraseology, we may have something like the following:

We generally reason: "A" is "A" because "A" is "A"; or "A" is "A", therefore, "A" is "A". Zen agrees or accepts this way of reasoning, but Zen has its own way which is ordinarily not at all acceptable. Zen would say: "A" is "A" because "A" is not "A"; or "A" is not "A"; therefore, "A" is "A".

Our thinking on the worldly level is: Everything has its cause; nothing is without its cause; the causation works on and in all things. But Zen will agree with some Christians when they declare that God created the world out of nothing, or that God willed and the world came

---

[1] Tung-shan Liang-chieh, 809–69. The founder of the Zen school partly bearing his name.
[2] *The Transmission of the Lamp*, Fas. XIV, under "Ungan Donjo "(Yun-yen T'an-sh'eng).

into existence, or that "To say that God created the world yesterday or tomorrow would be foolishness, for God created the world and everything in it in the one present Now."[1]

Mathematics has this: $0=0$, $1=1$, $1+1=2$, and so on. Zen has these too, but it has no objection to the following either: $0=1$, $0=2$, $1+1=3$, etc. Why? Because zero is infinity and infinity is zero. Is this not irrational and beyond our comprehension?

A geometrical circle has a circumference and just one centre, and no more or less. But Zen admits the existence of a circle that has no circumference nor centre and, therefore, has an infinite number of centres. As this circle has no centre and, therefore, a centre everywhere, every radius from such a centre is of equal length—that is, all are equally infinitely long. According to the Zen point of view, the universe is a circle without a circumference, and every one of us is the centre of the universe. To put it more concretely: I am the centre, I am the universe, I am the creator. I raise the hand and lo! there is space, there is time, there is causation. Every logical law and every metaphysical principle rushes in to confirm the reality of my hand.

4

History deals with time and so does Zen, but with this difference: While history knows nothing of timelessness, perhaps disposing of it as "fabrication", Zen takes time along with timelessness—that is to say, time in timelessness and timelessness in time. Zen lives in this contradiction. I say, "Zen lives." History shuns anything living, for the living man does not like to be grouped with the past, with the dead. He is altogether too much alive for the historian, who is used to digging up old, decayed

[1] *Meister Eckhart: A Modern Translation.* Raymond Bernard Blakney (New York and London: Harper & Brothers, 1941), p. 214.

things from the grave. It is different with Zen. Zen makes the dead live once more and talk their life anew, although in fact there is no resurrection in Zen, because there is no birth, no death; we all live in timelessness. *Chih* means to become aware of this grand fact, which, however, does not seem to concern the historians.

Science teaches us abstraction, generalization, and specialization. This has warped our view of human beings to the extent that we put aside the living concrete and substitute for it something dead, universal, abstract, and, for that reason, existentially non-being. Economists speak of the "economic man", and politicians of the "political man"; perhaps historians have produced the "historical man". These are all abstractions and fabrications. Zen has nothing to do with the dead, with abstractions, logic, and the past. I wonder would Hu Shih agree with me in this statement?

By this time, I hope my meaning is clear when I say that Zen is not exhausted by being cosily placed in a historical corner, for Zen is far more than history. History may tell much about Zen in its relation to other things or events, but it is all *about* Zen and not Zen in itself as every one of us lives it. Zen is, in a way, iconoclastic, revolutionary, as Hu Shih justly remarks, but we must insist that Zen is not that alone; Zen still stands outside the frame.

For instance, what is it that makes Zen iconoclastic and revolutionary? Why does Zen apparently like to indulge in the use of abusive terms, often highly sacrilegious, and to resort to unconventionalities, or to "the most profane language", even when they do not seem absolutely necessary? We cannot say that Zen followers wanted to be merely destructive and to go against everything that had been traditionally established. To state that Zen is revolutionary is not enough; we must probe into the reason that makes Zen act as it does. What is it, then, that incited Zen to be iconoclastic, revolutionary, unconventional, "profane", and, I say, irrational? Zen is not merely a negative movement. There is something very positive and affirmative about it. To find this, I may have to be a kind of historian myself.

Zen is really a great revolutionary movement in the world history of thought. It originated in China and, in my opinion, could not arise anywhere else. China has many things she can well be proud of. This I mean not in the sense of cultural nationalism but on the world level of the development of human consciousness. Until about the time of Hui-neng (died 713) Buddhism was still highly coloured with the Indian tint of abstract thinking. The Chinese achievements along this line were remarkable indeed, and I think such Buddhist philosophers as Chih-i and Fa-tsang are some of the greatest thinkers of the world. They were Chinese products, no doubt, but we may say that their way of thinking was stimulated by their Indian predecessors and that they were the direct descendants of Asvaghosa, Nagarjuna, Asanga, and others. But it was in Zen that the Chinese mind completely asserted itself, in a sense, in opposition to the Indian mind. Zen could not rise and flourish in any other land or among any other people. See how it swept over the Middle Kingdom throughout the T'ang and the Sung dynasties. This was quite a noteworthy phenomenon in the history of Chinese thought. What made Zen wield such a powerful moral, intellectual, and spiritual influence in China?

If any people or race is to be characterized in a word, I would say that the Chinese mind is eminently practical, in contrast to the Indian mind, which is speculative and tends toward abstraction and unworldliness and non-historical-mindedness. When the Buddhist monks first came to China the people objected to their not working and to their being celibate. The Chinese people reasoned: If those monks do not work, who will feed them? No other than those who are not monks or priests. The laymen will naturally have to work for non-working parasites. If the monks do not marry, who are going to look after their ancestral spirits? Indians took it for granted that the spiritual teachers would not engage in manual labour, and it was most natural for them to be dependent upon laymen for their food, clothing, and housing. It was beneath their dignity to work on the farm, to chop wood, to wash dishes. Under these social conditions Zen could not arise in India, for it is one of the most typical traits of Zen life that the masters and disciples work together in all kinds of manual activity and that, while thus working, they exchange their *mondo* on highly metaphysical subjects. They, however, carefully avoid using abstract terms. They utilize any concrete objects they find about them in order to be convinced of the universality of truth. If they are picking tea leaves, the plants themselves become the subject of discourse. If they are walking and notice objects such as birds or animals, the birds or animals are immediately taken up for a lively *mondo*. Not only things living or not-living but also the activities they manifest are appropriate matter for serious inquiry. For Zen masters, life itself with all its dynamism is eloquent expression of the *Tao*.

Therefore, if the master is found making his own straw sandals, or plastering the wall, or reading the *sutras*, or drinking tea, a monk will approach and ask questions. Likewise, when the master catches his disciples engaged in cutting grass, gathering wheat, carrying wood, pounding rice, or pushing a wheelbarrow, he presses them for answers by asking questions which are apparently innocent but are inwardly full of deep metaphysical or spiritual meaning. Joshu's[1] treating all equally with a cup of tea regardless of the monk's status is one of the most noted examples. The master may ask casually whence a monk comes and, according to the answer he advances, the master deals with the monk variously. Such may be called the practical lessons of Zen.

If Zen had developed along the intellectual line of speculation, this would never have happened. But Zen moves on *prajna*-intuition and is concerned with an absolute present in which the work goes on and life is lived.

[1] *The Transmission of the Lamp*, Fas. X, under "Chao-chou Ts'ung-shen".

Around this absolute present all Zen study is carried on. The moral value of anything or any work comes afterwards, and is the later development when the work already accomplished comes out as an object of study detached from the worker himself. The evaluation is secondary and not essential to the work itself while it is going on. Zen's daily life is to live and not to look at life from the outside —which would alienate life from the actual living of it. Then there will be words, ideas, concepts, etc., which do not belong in Zen's sphere of interest.

The question of profanity or sacredness, of decorum or indecency, is the result of abstraction and alienation. When a question comes up, Zen is no longer there but ten thousand miles away. The masters are not to be detained with idle discussions as to whether a thing is conventionally tabooed or not. Their objective is not iconoclasm, but their way of judging values comes out automatically as such from their inner life. The judgment which we, as outsiders, give them is concerned only with the bygone traces of the Zen life, with the corpse whose life has departed a long time ago. Zen thus keeps up its intimate contact with life. I would not say that the Indian mind is not like this, but rather that the Chinese mind is more earth-conscious and hates to be lifted up too high from the ground. The Chinese people are practical in this sense, and Zen is deeply infused with this spirit. Hui-neng never stopped pounding rice and chopping wood, and Pai-chang (Hyakujo)[1] was a great genius in organizing the Zen monastery on this principle of work.

5

Hu Shih is no doubt a brilliant writer and an astute thinker, but his logic of deducing the Zen methodology or irrationalism and "seeming craziness" out of the economic necessity of getting support from the powerful

[1] Ibid., Fas. VI, under "Pai-chang Hui-hai".

patrons is, to say the least, illogical and does not add to his rational historicism. While referring to "these new situations and probably many others", Hu Shih does not specify what those "probably many others" were. Probably he did not have time to go over the "historical setting" of those days when "many others" came up and forced the Zen masters to resort to their "mad technique" instead of carrying on the old method of "plain speaking".

But can we imagine that the Zen masters who really thought that there were no Buddhas and no *bodhisattvas*, or that, if there were any, they were no better than "murderers who would seduce innocent people to the pitfalls of the Devil", could not be free to refuse any form of patronage by the civil authorities? What logical connection could there be between the Zen masters courting the patronage of the powers and their invention of "some other subtle but equally thought-provoking way of expressing what the earlier masters had said outspokenly"?

Is the stick-swinging or the "Ho!" any subtler than the earlier masters' outspokenness? I wonder what makes Hu Shih think that the "Ho!" or "the stick" is not so "outspoken" but "seemingly crazy". To my mind, they —"Ho!" and "the stick"—are quite as outspoken, plain speaking, as saying "No Buddhas!", "No clinging to anything!", etc. Yes, if anything, they are more expressive, more efficient, more to the point than so-called "plain and unmistakable *language*". There is nothing "crazy" about them, seemingly or not seemingly. They are, indeed, one of the sanest methodologies one can use for either demonstrating or instructing students. Is it not silly to ask what a Buddha is when the questioner himself is one? What can an impatient master do to make the questioner realize the fact? An argument leads to a series of arguments. There is nothing more effective and short-cut than giving the questioner the "thirty blows" or a hearty "Ho!". Though much may depend on the questioner and the situation which brings him to the master, the master does very well in appealing to this "seemingly crazy" method. It goes without saying that the "Ho!" and "the stick" do not always mean the same thing. They have a variety of uses, and it will take a deep Zen insight to comprehend what they mean in different situations. Rinzai (Lin-chi I-hsuan), for example, distinguishes four kinds of "Ho!".

Now let me ask who are the "earlier masters" referred to by Hu Shih? Rinzai spoke outspokenly, and so did Tokusan (Te-shan Hsuan-chien), as is confirmed by Hu Shih himself. And it was they who used the stick and uttered "Ho!". Historically, in this they are preceded by Baso (Ma-tsu), who used the fist too. The history of the "crazy" pedagogic methodology of Zen may be said to start with Baso. Sekito (Shih-t'ou), his contemporary, also noted for his Zen insight and understanding, was not as "mad" as Baso, but the spread of Zen all over China, especially in the South, dates from Baso "in the west of the River" and Sekito "in the south of the Lake". Hu Shih's "earlier masters" must be those earlier than Baso and Sekito, which means Jinne (Shen-hui) and Yeno (Hui-neng), Nangaku Yejo (Nan-yueh Hui-jang), Seigen Gyoshi (Ch'ing-yuan), etc. But Hu Shih evidently classes Rinzai, Tokusan, and Baso among those Zen masters who expounded Zen in plain outspoken language.

Hu Shih does not understand what *pu shuo po* (in translation, "do not tell outwardly") really means. It is not just not to speak plainly. I wish he would remember that there is something in the nature of *prajna*-intuition which eludes every attempt at intellectualization and rejects all plain speaking, so called. It is not purposely shunning this way of expression. As *prajna*-intuition goes beyond the two horns of a dilemma, it grudges committing itself to either side. This is what I mean when I say that Zen is beyond the ken of human understanding; by understanding, I mean conceptualization. When the Zen-experience—or *prajna*-intuition, which is the same thing— is brought to conceptualization, it is no more the experience itself; it turns into something else. *Pu shuo po* is not a pedagogical method; it is inherent in the constitution of the experience, and even the Zen master cannot do anything with it.

To illustrate my point, I will quote two *mondo*. The subject of both is the ancient mirror, but one appears to be diametrically opposed to the other in its statement.

A monk asked: "When the ancient mirror is not yet polished, what statement can we make about it?"
The master answered: "The ancient mirror."
The monk: "What do we have after it is polished?"
The master: "The ancient mirror."
When the same question was brought to another master, he answered to the first: "Heaven and earth are universally illumined." To the second, "Pitch dark" was given as the answer.

The ancient mirror is the ultimate reality, the God-head, the mind, the undifferentiated totality. "When it is polished" means the differentiation, the world created by God, the universe of the ten thousand things. In the first *mondo* the mirror remains the same whether it is polished or not. In the second *mondo*, when it is not polished or differentiated, it illumines the whole universe, but when it is polished it loses its ancient brilliance and the light is hidden behind the multitudinousness of things. We may say that the second *mondo* directly contradicts the first, or that the first ignores the fact of differentiation, which is not rational. We can raise more questions concerning each singly and the two in their relationship. But *pu shuo po*; it takes too long to discuss the point fully in order to satisfy our understanding. When all is done, the original intuition from which we started is lost sight of; in fact, we do not know exactly where we are, so thickly covered are we with the dust of argument. The use of "plain language" which we aimed at in the beginning puts us now in the maze of intellection and gives us nothing solid; we are all vaporized.

Chu Hsi was a great Confucian thinker—there is no doubt about that. But he had no *prajna*-intuition into the constitution of the ancient mirror. Therefore, what he says about *pu shuo po* and also about "the golden needle" working underneath the embroidery is off the track. There is nothing pedagogical here. As to *pu shuo po* (unexplainable), I have *shuo po liao* (explained away) as above.

Now as regards the golden needle. It is not that the needle is designedly held back from the sight of the outsider. It cannot be delivered to him even when you want that done. It is something each of us has to get by himself. It is not that "I'll not pass it on to you", but "I can't pass it on to you". For we are all in possession of a golden needle which, however, becomes our own only when we discover it in the unconscious. What can be passed on from one person to another is not native to him who gets it.

Hsing-yen's (Kyogen's) story may be illuminating in this connection.[1]

Hsing-yen Chih-hsian was a disciple of I-san (Kweishan Ling-yu, 771–834). Recognizing his aptitude for Zen, I-san once asked Kyogen (Hsing-yen): "I am not going to find out how much you know from book-learning and other sources. What I want you to tell me is this: Can you let me have a word (*i chu*) from you before you came out of your mother's body, before you came to discriminate things?"

"A word" (*i chu*) is something one cannot *shuo po* (explain fully) however much one may try; nor is it a thing which one can pass on to another. Zen wants us to grasp this, each in his own way, out of the depths of consciousness, even before this becomes psychologically or biologically possible. It is therefore beyond the scope of our relative understanding. How can we do it? Yet this is what I-san, as a good Zen master, demanded of his disciple.

Kyogen did not know how to answer or what to say. After being absorbed in deep meditation for some time, he presented his views. But they were all rejected by the master. He then

---

[1] *The Transmission of the Lamp*, Fas. XI.

asked I-san to let him have the right answer. I-san said : "What
I can tell you is my understanding and is of no profit to you."
Kyogen returned to his room and went over all his notes, in
which he had many entries, but he could not find anything
suitable for his answer. He was in a state of utter despondency.
"A painted piece of cake does not appease the hungry man." So
saying, he committed all his note-books to the fire. He decided
not to do anything with Zen, which he now thought to be
above his abilities. He left I-san and settled down at a temple
where there was the tomb of Chu Kokushi (Chung, the
National Teacher). One day while sweeping the ground,
his broom made a stone strike a bamboo, which made a noise;
and this awoke his unconscious consciousness, which he had
even before he was born. He was delighted and grateful to
his teacher I-san for not having *shuo chueh* (explained) what
the *i chu* (word) was. The first lines of the *gatha* he then
composed run as follows:

> "One blow has made me forget all my learning;
> There was no need for specific training and cultivation."

When I-san did not explain the *i chu* for Kyogen he
had no thought of educating him by any specific device.
He could not do anything, even if he wished, for his
favourite disciple. As he then told him, whatever he
would say was his own and not anybody else's. Knowledge can be transmitted from one person to another, for
it is a common possession of the human community, but
Zen does not deal in such wares. In this respect Zen is
absolutely individualistic.

There is one thing I would like to add which will help
to clarify Hu Shih's idea of Chinese Zen.

Hu Shih must have noticed in his historical study of
Zen in China that Zen has almost nothing to do with the
Indian Buddhist practice of *dhyana*, though the term Zen
or Ch'an is originally derived from the Sanskrit. The
meaning of Zen as meditation or quiet thinking or contemplation no longer holds good after Hui-neng (Yeno),
the sixth Patriarch. As I have said, it was Hui-neng's
revolutionary movement that achieved this severance.

Hui-neng's message to Chinese Buddhism was the identity of *prajna* and *dhyana*. Shen-hui (Jinne) was most expressive in giving voice to this theme. He was more intellectual in his understanding of Zen than Baso, Sekito, and others, and this was one of the reasons why Shen-hui's school lost its hold on the Chinese mind. The Chinese mind does not tend to be intellectual or metaphysical, and Zen, as the native product of the Chinese mentality, abhors this strain of intellectuality in its study. The Rinzai way of handling Zen is in better accord with the spirit of Zen and goes well with the Chinese liking for practicality and going direct to the objective. At all events, the essential character of Zen, which is based on the identity of *prajna* and *dhyana*, was pointed out in quite an intelligible manner by Shen-hui, as described in the preceding pages.

Before Hui-neng, this problem of the relationship between *dhyana* and *prajna* was not so sharply brought to a focus in China. The Indian mind naturally tended to emphasize *dhyana* more than *prajna*, and Chinese Buddhists followed their Indian predecessors without paying much attention to the subject. But when Hui-neng came on the scene he at once perceived that *prajna* was the most essential thing in the study of Buddhism, and that as long as *dhyana* practice was brought forward at the expense of *prajna* the real issue was likely to be neglected. Moreover, *dhyana* came to be mixed up with *samatha* and *vipasyana*, tranquillization and contemplation, which were a great concern of followers of the Tendai (T'ien-t'ai) school. I do not think Hui-neng was historically conscious of these things; he simply wanted to proclaim his *prajna*-intuition. The situation was accentuated when Shen-hsiu, or, rather, his followers, loudly protested against the Hui-neng movement, which was headed by Shen-hui (Jinne). There are still many Buddhist scholars who are confused about Chinese Zen and the Indian Buddhist practice of *dhyana*.

There are more points I should like to take up for discussion here, but they will have to wait for another occasion. Let me hope that the foregoing pages have dispelled whatever misunderstanding Hu Shih holds in regard to what Zen is *in itself* apart from its historical setting.

# VI. MONDO

ONE of the most characteristic features of Zen methodology of teaching is what is known as *mondo*. *Mondo* (*wen-ta* in Chinese) literally means "question (and) answer". It is a dialogue taking place between two persons, generally between a master and a disciple. The latter, however, may not always be a disciple, for *mondo* frequently takes place between any two or more persons.

A *mondo* differs from a dialogue in this way: As typically represented by "Plato's Dialogues" or "Buddha's Dialogues", a dialogue is a series of questions and answers. But a Zen *mondo* is short, abrupt, and not at all serial. It is what logically follows from the nature of Zen-experience itself. Zen is not a philosophy, not a network of ideas, not the unfolding of a concept. As is stated by the Zen masters, it is directly or immediately pointing to the mind. It refuses to resort to any medium to make itself known. But as long as we are human and social, we cannot help making use of something to express ourselves. Zen masters cannot escape this human conditionality. Hence the evolution of Zen *mondo*.

But as soon as Zen appeals to language to express itself it inevitably becomes the victim of all the inconveniences, all the restrictions, and all the contradictions which are inherent in language. *Mondo* tries to reduce these shortcomings to a minimum. This is one of the reasons it is cast in an epigrammatic and enigmatic mould of expression, thereby cutting short the liability of its growing serially or discursively.

*Mondo*, however, is not of a uniform character; it varies indefinitely according to situations and personalities. The following are examples mainly culled from a book entitled *The Transmission of the Lamp* (*Dentoroku* in Japanese), which contains a rich treasure of Zen *mondo*.

A monk of the Sung dynasty called Chosui Shisen

(Chang-shui Tzu-hsuan)[1] once asked a Zen master called Roya Ekaku:

"The Originally Pure—how can the mountains and the rivers and great earth come out of it?"

The master answered: "The Originally Pure—how can the mountains and the rivers and great earth come out of it?"

"The Originally Pure" is the Absolute or the Godhead. In Buddhism the Pure means being free from or devoid of all forms of particularization, and when it is predicated by "originally", the Pure is expressed in terms of time. The Originally Pure, therefore, means the Godhead who is in the state of absolute transcendence. Now the question is: "How can this world of multitudes come out of the Godhead? How can the One produce 'the ten thousand things'?" In other words, what is the relationship of being to becoming?

This is the great metaphysical problem. When it is theologically stated, it touches the foundation of all religious systems, we might say. And Zen is naturally very much concerned with it too. But in this *mondo* above cited the answer is merely the question repeated. Superficially, it can hardly be called even a *mondo*, "question (and) answer", for there is nothing apparently corresponding to what we call an answer from our ordinary rationalistic point of view. But Chosui, who asked this question, is recorded to have had a *satori* ("understanding").

What does all this mean?

To make it fully intelligible to most of us who are relatively minded would mean to write a good-sized book. I will not go any further here than to raise such questions as the following and see what will come out of them: What made God think of creating a world at all? How did he come to conceive the idea of uttering: "Let there be light"? The answer is beyond human calculation. To understand God's will or thought one has to be God himself. And, moreover, what makes us think of asking God's intention—if the creation had any such thing as to be

called intention behind it—may not this asking itself
come out of God's will? Is it not God himself who prompts
us to ask about his intention or will? If this be the case,
the one who can answer the question must be God himself.
When we ask such a question as if it came out of ourselves
and not from the Creator, are we not putting ourselves
on the wrong track? The answer and the question come
out of the same root. Therefore, when the root of the
question is taken hold of, the answer is already in our
hands without our being conscious of the fact.

When the questioner questions himself, he has already
answered himself, for the questioning is no other than the
answering. God by creating a world answers his own
question. Chosui understood his question when he saw it
echoed back in the form of his own question. This echoing
is the answer. If there were no echoing, there would be
no answering the question. The knocking at the door is
answered by its being opened. In fact, the knocking is
the opening. John calls out to Harry, and Harry responds. The calling is the responding. When this is understood there is Zen.

*Mondo*, then, means mutuality, or co-responding. As
long as the Originally Pure remains pure, that is, remains
with itself and in itself and does not ask any question,
there is no splitting, hence no answering, no mutuality,
no "participation". When any question comes out at all,
it sees itself reflected in the form of "the ten thousand
things", in the form of "the mountains and the rivers and
the great earth". Here is neither coming-out nor coming-
in. The Originally Pure is no other than "the mountains
and the rivers and the great earth". When the Pure calls
out, the echo responds; the mountains rise, the rivers
flow, and the great earth moves. God now sees himself
in the mirror of "the ten thousand things". The questioning is setting up the mirror.

When Tozan (Tung-shan) came to Shozan Yecho
(Shu-shan Hui-ch'ao),[1] Yecho said: "What makes you
come here when you are already a recognized leader?"

[1] *Zoku Dentoroku*, Fas. IX.

Tozan: "I still have my doubt which I am unable to solve. Hence my appearance here."

Yecho then called out to Tozan: "O Ryokai!" (Ryokai was Tozan's name). Tozan responded: "Yes, Sir."

Yecho: "What is that?"

Tozan gave no answer.

Thereupon Yecho remarked: "A fine Buddha has no halo!"

Buddha with a halo or with no halo is standing before Yecho. But there is one thing it is better for us to remember. When we become conscious of the halo, the halo vanishes. Not only does it vanish, but it is apt to harm us in one way or another. The halo shines most when we are unconscious of it. But as human beings endowed with all the functions of consciousness, we must at least once become conscious of it. Becoming conscious of it, however, the best thing we can do with it is to forget it altogether. To be always remembering it is to cling to it and the clinging does us a great deal of harm. Let us, therefore, remember it as if not remembering—that is, be unconsciously conscious of it.

Joshu (Ch'ao-chou Ts'ung-shen),[1] a grand old master of the T'ang dynasty, once gave this warning to his pupils: "Do not linger where there is Buddha. Pass quickly by where there is no Buddha." Why is he so antagonistic to Buddha as he apparently is? Another time he said: "Wash your mouth thoroughly if you say 'Buddha'." Is the word "Buddha" so defiling and infectious? When you are conscious of a halo, this is what happens. The old masters are kind-hearted if they appear so forbidding.

When Daizui (Tai-shui Fa-chen)[2] was staying with Isan, he distinguished himself in various ways, in discipline, industry, and daily behaviour. The master Isan thought a great deal of him. One day Isan called him in and asked: "You have been here for some time, but you have never approached me with a question. How is that?"

[1] *Goto Yegen*, Fas. IV. The title means "Essentials of the Five Lamps".
[2] Ibid.

Daizui: "But where do you want me to insert a word?"

Isan: "Why do you not ask what 'Buddha is'?"

Daizui lost no time in vigorously applying his hand over Isan's mouth.

Isan: "You have really attained the marrow."

Isan is somewhat too "grandmotherly", as the Zen man would remark. Why not give a hearty blow of a stick to Daizui, who behaves as if he knew a thing or two? But he might have given to Isan a similar treatment even before Isan told him what to ask.

A monk asked: "What is my mind?" The master answered: "Who is asking?" When you utter a word, "it" is no more there. But if you do not, how could you ever come to a realization? The asking is important indeed, but let us remember that the asking is really putting another head over the one you already have. God would not be God if he had not created the world with all its joys and woes—this would be my answer if I were a Christian and were asked why God created the world. Indeed, he is a fool who asks such a question. For he would have to go from one master to another till the end of his life if he once started asking these questions: What is the Mind? What is the Self? What is God? What is Buddha?

The following *mondo* took place between Shoshu (Shao-hsiu of Lung-chi-shan),[1] the master, and a monk.

Monk: "What is my eternal Mind?" Master: "Did you ever ask Kagyoku?" The monk: "I do not understand." Master: "If you do not understand, go to Sozan at the end of the summer and ask him."

I will now initiate you into another type of *mondo* where the question of affirmation and negation is treated. Here is a kind of Zen-dialectic. But there is no trace here of the dialectical argument which we generally see in a treatise of Western philosophy. As you know, Zen is not logic nor is it given up to metaphysical discourse. That is why *mondo* is a characteristic of Zen.

A company of monks came, and Daizui asked: "What would those who have mastered Zen call East?"

[1] *Zoku Dentoroku*, Fas. XXIV.

The monks' leader answered: "It is not to be called East."

Daizui shouted: "O you dirty-smelling ass! If you do not call it East, what do you call it?" There was no answer.[1]

The monks' leader is all right when he answers: "It is not to be called East." Daizui is also right when he abuses him by calling him an ill-smelling ass when the leader answers: "East is not East." For what else could East be called? According to us ordinary-minded people, East is East and West is West. This is the agreement we have reached since the beginning of civilization. If East ceases to be East and West West there will surely be all kinds of topsyturvydom, and it will be impossible for any one of us to walk or drive safely in the streets of London or elsewhere. Perhaps even our living will be endangered, because the sun will not rise any longer from the East and set in the West. Night will be day and day will be night. My pen will slip out of my hand and turn into yours. Either I am thus stealing your property, or you are losing your sense of identity—and this is no exaggeration. For when East is not East, not only our system of spatial references but also that of temporal fixations comes to an end. When we cannot even move a finger, we cannot go on living for a moment, and for this same reason we can never die. For there is no such thing as death. Is it not wonderful to see that this innocent-sounding little *mondo* can contain in it such a ruinous logical consequence, involving a problem of life and death?

We now can fully realize that a most unexpectedly consequential thought is concealed under a most trifling matter-of-fact kind of statement. Zen *mondo* cannot be set aside as of no meaning. We are indeed to weigh every word or gesture that comes from a Zen master.

Probably a few words are necessary to make clear what I mean here.

When the Godhead asserted himself, he became a

[1] *Zoku Dentoroku*, Fas. XI.

God, which was the negation of himself. The Godhead
ceased to be the Godhead in order to be himself. An
affirmation always implies a negation, and a negation an
affirmation; they are interrelated. One cannot be had
without the other. "A" is to be "not-A" when "A" wills
to be "A". The willing is possible only by negating itself.
The Godhead cannot help being a creator. But as soon
as he creates he is no more himself; there is the creator
and the created.

The Zen master produces a rosary and asks his disciples: "If you call it a rosary you touch, and if you do
not, you 'go against'. Without committing yourself to
either, what do you call it?"

"To touch" is to assert, and "to go against" is to
negate. What the master wants us to say here is "the one
word" which is in the beginning, that is, in the beginningless beginning, and which, therefore, never vanishes away
at the end of the world which is really no end. This "one
word" is beyond yes and no, beyond East and West,
beyond rosary and no-rosary, beyond "touching" and
"going against". When Daizui rebuked the monk who
denied "East" as "an ill-smelling ass", Daizui meant that
the monk had not yet realized what is beyond affirmation
and negation, that the monk was yet far from grasping
"the one word".

You will naturally ask now what is this "one word".
Indeed, when one has it, one has all the secrets of being and
of creation. The following *mondo* is what you want to solve.

Shobi (Ch'u-wei of Ch'ien-chou)[1] asked Kyozan:
"What is your name?"

Kyozan: "Ye-jaku."

Shobi: "What is 'ye'? what is 'jaku'?"

Kyozan: "Right before you."

Shobi: "Still there is a before-and-after (relation)."

Kyozan: "Let us for a while put aside the question of
a before-and-after (relation). O master, what do you
see?"

Shobi: "Have a cup of tea."

[1] *Zoku Dentoroku*, Fas. IX.

To make this *mondo* somewhat reasonable, supposing it to be possible, to those who have not yet been ushered into the way of Zen, I have to add a few words. Now it is customary for the Zen master to ask a newcomer to his monastery such questions as these:

(1) "Where do you come from?" (2) "Where are you going?" (3) "What is your name?"

The first and second questions are concerned with the whence and whither of our existence, while the third is the question of existence itself. The Zen master's "whence?" does not always refer to our tridimensional spatial relations. So with "whither?" it does not point to the destination of the monk's itinerary. But at the same time it would be well for us to remember that Zen abhors our ordinary habit of dealing with mere abstractions.

In the present *mondo* Shobi asks the name of the monk, and when it is given he dissects it into its component parts. *Ye* literally means "transcendental wisdom", which is the Chinese equivalent of the Sanskrit *prajna*, and *jaku* is "peace" or "tranquillity". The combination is, therefore, "the peace of transcendental wisdom", or "the tranquillity of the Originally Pure", which is quite a suitable name for a Zen monk. There is no need for the master to propose a second question about the meaning of each word, *ye* and *jaku*, for he knows perfectly well what they literally denote. Therefore, when he asks again, naturally he has something more in his mind than just asking the question. He intends to see what understanding Kyozan, the monk, has about Zen. Kyozan is no novice; he surely would not try to tell Shobi what *ye* is, what *jaku* is. He knows perfectly what Shobi is driving after. Hence his answer: "Right before you."

"Transcendental wisdom" or "the Originally Pure" is not something to be explained in words; it is not an idea about which something could be affirmed or denied. A person who is designated as "Ye-jaku" on the plane of relativity and individualism is standing right in front of another person who is referred to as Shobi in the vocabulary of this world of particulars. This is, however, an

English way of saying it. In the original Chinese there is no reference to any particular object or subject. Literally translated it simply reads: "Only-is-eye's before." In English this does not make sense, for we shall demand before whose eye or eyes it is, and who is before whom. All these references are to be definitely stated. In Chinese or Japanese the pronouns or the objects represented by them are omitted, which frequently leads to obscurity. But, as in the present case, this obscurity is the description of a precise situation in which they, Shobi and Kyozan, are finding themselves. "The Originally Pure" is there without its being specifically located here or there and timed now or then. It is before somebody's eye, which means anybody's and everybody's eye—that is, wherever there is an eye to see. "It is just before the eye" is quite expressive of the actuality which both, Shobi and Kyozan, were facing at the time of the *mondo*.

But as soon as language intrudes itself in one form or another, the question of time and space and causal sequence comes in. Hence Shobi's charge about the relationship of before and after. Kyozan Yejaku was, however, quick enough to catch Shobi's way of looking at the matter. Kyozan immediately demanded: "O master, what do you see?" This counter-questioning is characteristic of Zen. Instead of directly answering the question, Kyozan wanted to know what Shobi saw before and after him. There is a subtle point in it. For as long as there is any seeing the question arises as to who sees and what is seen and consequently the question of before-and-after.

When a *mondo* comes to this pass, there must be a turning point which puts an end to the whole procedure. When intellectualization develops, Zen turns into philosophy. It was natural for Shobi to avoid this pitfall. He concluded the *mondo* in a dramatic and yet an appropriate way: "Have a cup of tea."

As long as we stay at the level of relativity or intellectualization, we shall have all kinds of disagreement and have to keep up a series of hot discussions. This is inevitable. Zen fully realizes it and wants us all to go back to living itself, where there will be no more arguments, no more controversies. But here is a most important matter we must not forget to mention in this connection. Zen does not just demand living without involving ourselves in logical complications. Zen demands that we have a certain experience of awareness as we go on living, for this awareness is what makes us humans qualitatively different from all other forms of living being. And it is here indeed that we humans, regardless of all sorts of differentiation which are discernible among us, find our ultimate abode of peace, which is also our original home where we all come from and where we all long to be back. This is where we all can happily "take a cup of tea" with no "before-after", with no "whence-whither", with no "I am-thou art".

In passing I wish to remind my readers that our sitting quietly and sipping tea together on the common ultimate ground of living realities does not by any means hinder our being infinitely differentiated from one another, and also our possibly being engaged in a never-ending series of arguments.

There is a famous story which it may be interesting to quote in connection with Shobi's "Have a cup of tea". Joshu Jushin[1] was a great master of Zen in the middle period of the T'ang dynasty. One day a new monk arrived at his monastery. He asked: "Have you ever been here before?" When the monk answered: "No, master, this is my first visit," Joshu said: "Have a cup of tea." Later, there was another monk who came to see Joshu. Joshu asked: "Have you been here before?" The monk said: "Yes, master." Joshu said: "Have a cup of tea."

The Inju (the manager of the monastery) approached Joshu and asked: "How is it that you ask the two monks in the same way to take a cup of tea regardless of their different ways of answering? One says that he has never been here before, and you tell him to have a cup of tea; while the other says that he has been here and you tell

[1] *Goto Yegen*, Fas. IV.

him just as before to have a cup of tea. I fail to understand you, O master."

When Joshu was thus asked by the Inju, Joshu called out: "O Inju!" And the Inju at once responded: "Yes, master." Joshu lost no time in saying: "Have a cup of tea, O Inju."

"Have a cup of tea" is thus uniformly given to all who approach the master, no matter what attitude they assume toward him. Affirmation or negation, yes or no, a spade or not a spade, they are all no more than verbal differentiation. As long as we remain in the realm of verbalism, a dialogue is needed. But once out of it, *mondo* is the only way the Zen masters can make use of the expression of their experience.

Let me conclude this with a few more examples of *mondo* by Daido.

Question: "I am told that one reality universally moistens all beings. What is one reality?" Answer: "It is raining."

"Moistening" is an allusion to a story in the *Saddharma-pundarika Sutra* where Buddha explains how one rain uniformly moistens all plants and makes them grow each in accordance with its nature, the pine as pine, the chrysanthemum as chrysanthemum. Hence the master's answer: "It is raining."

Question: "It is said that one particle of dust contains all the worlds. How is this?"

Answer: "The one has already turned into several particles."

Question: "How about the golden chain when it has not yet been broken up?"

Answer: "It is broken up."

# VII. THE ROLE OF NATURE IN
# ZEN BUDDHISM

AT THE outset it is advisable to know what we mean by Nature, for the term is ambiguous and has been used in various senses. Let me here just mention a few of the ideas associated in the Western mind with Nature.

The first thing is that Nature is contrasted with God; the natural stands on the one hand against the divine. Nature is something working against what is godly, and in this sense often means "creation" or "the earth". God created the world, but strangely the world goes against him, and God is found fighting against his own creation.

The adjective "natural", while in one sense standing in contrast to the divine, in another sense accords with it. When "naturalness" is used in contrast to artificiality it acquires something of the divine. Childlikeness is often compared to godliness. Child life has more in it of godliness than adult life, being much closer to Nature. God, then, is not altogether absent in Nature.

When we contrast Nature with Man, we emphasize the physical, material aspect of Nature rather than its moral or spiritual aspect, which is pre-eminently involved when we contrast it with God. Nature has thus two aspects as we humans view it. Inasmuch as it is "natural", it is godly; but when it is material it functions against human spirituality or godliness, whatever that may mean. As long as Nature is regarded as the material world, as our senses perceive it, it is something we want to conquer. Nature here faces us as a kind of power, and wherever there is the notion of power it is connected with that of conquest. For Man, therefore, Nature is to be conquered and made use of for his own material welfare and comfort. Nature affords him a variety of opportunities to develop his powers, but at the same time there is always on the part of Man the tendency to exploit and abuse it for his selfish ends.

．　　　．　　　．　　　．　　　．

The Nature-Man dichotomy issues, as I think, from the Biblical account in which the Creator is said to have given mankind the power to dominate all creation. It is fundamentally due to this story that Western people talk so much about conquering Nature. When they invent a flying machine they say they have conquered the air; when they climb to the top of Mt. Everest they loudly announce that they have succeeded in conquering the mountain. This idea of conquest comes from the relationship between Nature and Man being regarded as that of power, and this relationship involves a state of mutual opposition and destruction.

This power-relationship also brings out the problem of rationality. Man is rational, whereas Nature is brutal, and Man strives to make Nature amenable to his idea of rationality. Rationality is born with the rising of consciousness out of the primordial Unconscious. Consciousness makes it possible for the human being to reflect upon his own doings and the events around him. This reflection gives him the power to rise above mere naturalness and to bring it under his control.

There is no discipline in Nature because it operates blindly. Discipline, which is something human and artificial, and to that extent works for bad as well as for good, belongs entirely to humankind. As long as he is capable of it, Man trains himself for a definite purpose.

Nature, on the other hand, is purposeless, and it is because of this purposelessness that Nature in one sense is "conquered" by Man and in another sense conquers Man. For however purposeful Man may be, he does not know ultimately whither he is going, and his pride has after all no substance whatever.

In this paper, then, let us understand Nature as something antithetical to what is ordinarily known as divine;

as something irrational yet amenable to our mechanical, economic, utilitarian treatment; as something not human, not in possession of human feelings, and devoid of moral significance; as something which finally overpowers Man in spite of Man's partial and temporary success. In short, Nature is brutally factual, with no history objectively set before us and to be regarded as commercially exploitable, but finally swallowing us all in the purposelessness of the Unknown.

Concretely speaking, Nature consists of mountains and rivers, grass and trees, stones and earth, suns, moons and stars, birds and animals. Nature is all that constitutes what is commonly known as Man's objective world.

## 2

When Nature is seen in this light it may seem well defined, but Nature has a great deal more to say to us. Nature is indeed an eternal problem, and when it is solved, we know not only Nature but ourselves; the problem of Nature is the problem of human life.

From the human point of view, anything that is not of human origin may be said to be of Nature. But Man is, after all, part of Nature itself. First of all, Man himself is not Man-made but Nature-made, as much as anything we regard as of Nature. If so, what is Man-made? There is nothing in Man that does not belong in Nature. All things Man-made must be considered Nature-made and not Man-made. If God created the world, he created Man as part of it. God did not create Man as something separate from Nature so that Man can stand outside Nature as a controlling power and have things "Man-made" put against things "Nature-made".

But as far as the Biblical account is concerned, Man was made in God's image and Nature was to be dominated by Man.[1] And this idea is the real beginning of human tragedy. I wish to ask if it is the right way of

[1] Genesis i, 27–8.

thinking—this idea of domination. For when the idea of power, which is domination, comes in, all kinds of struggles arise, and as this struggle is always ego-centred its outcome is tragic.

Nature, as we have seen, includes all "created" things. To think that these are all under human control is altogether illogical and cannot be consistently maintained. But Western people unconsciously follow this idea and their moral attitude towards Nature is thereby determined. Man, though made in God's image, has his own way of doing things, which is by no means God's way. For this reason he was expelled from Eden. He is now partly God's and partly Satan's child, and what he does quite frequently contradicts the divine commands and also sometimes his own self-interest. As to Nature, it also acts against God, though it cannot be anything else but God's creation.

Man is against God, Nature is against God, and Man and Nature are against each other. If so, God's own likeness (Man), God's own creation (Nature), and God himself—all three are at war. But with our human way of thinking, God did not create the world just to see it revolt against himself and make it fight within itself.

From another point of view, however, it is in the nature of things that as soon as there is a world of the many there is conflict. When the world is once out of God's hand, he cannot control it; it is sure to revolt and fight in every possible way. So we have now Nature against God and Man against Nature and God.

In Biblical terms Nature is the "flesh", "lust of the flesh", "sinful flesh", etc. This brings the fight between Nature and Man to a more concrete and sensuous level. The human body, which is a mixture of God and Nature, becomes a most bloody fighting arena for these two forces.

From these considerations we can summarize the Western attitude towards Nature thus:

(1) Nature is something hostile to Man and drags him down when he is struggling to reach God. The temptations of Nature symbolized as "the flesh" are often

irresistible and make Man exclaim: "The spirit is willing
but the flesh is weak."[1]

(2) While Nature and God are warring against each
other, Nature and Man are also at war. Or rather, as
commanded by God, Man is always striving to exercise
his dominating power over Nature.

(3) There is no way for Man to approach Nature in a
conciliatory, friendly spirit. One works to destroy the
other. There is nothing in Nature that will help Man in
his spiritual advancement.

(4) Nature is a material world and the material
world is meant for exploration and exploitation.

(5) In another sense the material world is brute fact,
stands as the *pour-soi* against the *en-soi*. Intellect cannot do
anything with it, but has to take it as it is and make the
best of it.

(6) The dichotomy of Nature-and-Man implies hostility, even an utter irreconcilability, and is, therefore,
mutually destructive.

(7) No idea seems to be present here which indicates
or even suggests human participation in, or identification
with, Nature. To the Western mind Nature and Man are
separate.

### 3

Man relies on Nature for food and cannot help being
influenced by Nature. He finds himself engaged in farm-
ing, hunting, fishing, etc., and each of these engagements
contributes to his character, for Nature cannot be conceived as a merely passive substance upon which Man
works. Nature is also power and energy; Nature reacts to
human calls. When Man is agreeable and in conformity
with Nature's way, it will co-operate with Man and
reveal to him all its secrets and even help him to understand himself. Each of us as a farmer or hunter or car-
penter gets from Nature what he looks for in it and

[1] Matthew xxvi, 41.

assimilates it in his own field. To this extent, Nature remoulds human character.

To treat Nature as something irrational and in opposition to human "rationality" is a purely Western idea, and sometimes we feel the proposition ought to be reversed. It is irrational of Man to try to make Nature obey his will, because Nature has its own way of carrying on its work which is not always Man's way, and Man has no right to impose his way upon Nature.

Nature, it is true, lacks consciousness. It is just the reed and not "a thinking reed". Because of this lack of consciousness it is regarded by Man as brute fact, as something with no will and intelligence of its own. It knows of nothing but an absolute "must", and permits no human interference except in its "must" way. It knows no favouritism and refuses to deviate from its course of inevitability. It is not accommodating; it is Man who must accommodate himself to Nature. Nature's "must" is absolute, and Man must accept it. In this respect Nature has something of the divine will.

This is the reason, I think, why being natural or spontaneous has an alluring quality in it. When a child performs deeds which polite society would condemn as undignified or improper or even immoral, the offences are not only condoned but accepted as acts of innocent childlikeness. There is something divine in being spontaneous and not being hampered by human conventionalities and their artificial hypocrisies. There is something direct and fresh in this lack of restraint by anything human, which suggests a divine freedom and creativity. Nature never deliberates; it acts directly out of its own heart, whatever this may mean. In this respect Nature is divine. Its "irrationality" transcends human doubts or ambiguities, and in our submitting to it, or rather accepting it, we transcend ourselves.

This acceptance or transcendence is a human prerogative. We accept Nature's "irrationality" or its "must" deliberately, quietly, and whole-heartedly. It is not a deed of blind and slavish submission to the inevitable.

It is an active acceptance, a personal willingness with no thought of resistance. In this there is no force implied, no resignation, but rather participation, assimilation, and perhaps in some cases even identification.

4

Nature is sometimes treated by Western people as something already "there" into which Man comes, and which he finds himself confronting, with hostility, because he feels he does not belong in it. He is conscious of a situation in which he is surrounded by all kinds of inert matter and brute fact. He does not know why he is there, nor does he realize what is coming to him. Endowed with consciousness, however, he thinks he can decide his future course, and he feels entirely responsible for his decision. He is lonely and helpless because Nature is threatening and ready to swallow him down into its own maw. He is overawed and trembles, not knowing what is best to do. This is the position, according to some modern thinkers, when Man encounters Nature. Here is no room for God to enter, but the dichotomy of Man and Nature is still maintained and in a more acutely oppressive relationship. Nature is brute fact and has nothing in common with Man. Man makes use of it economically with no sense of kinship with it, hence with no sense of gratitude or sympathetic affiliation.

Nature is here an unknown quantity, unfriendly and ready to frustrate Man's attempt to dominate it. Nature promises nothing but sheer emptiness. Whatever Man may build upon it is doomed to destruction. It is for this reason that modern men are constantly assailed with feelings of fear, insecurity, and anxiety.

There is, however, another way of considering Nature and Man. Inasmuch as Nature stands before Man as an unknown quantity and Man comes to it with his consciousness from somewhere else than Nature, Nature and Man cannot be friendly and sociable, for they have no way to communicate. They are strangers. But the very fact that Man finds himself encountering Nature demonstrates that the two are not unknown to each other. To this extent, then, Nature is already telling Man something of itself and Man is to that extent understanding Nature. Then Man cannot be said to be entirely an outsider but somehow stands in relation to Nature; perhaps comes out of Nature itself. Man must be after all an insider.

## 5

Here there is room for Zen Buddhism to enter, and to give its own views on the relationship of Nature and Man.

While separating himself from Nature, Man is still a part of Nature, for the fact of separation itself shows that Man is dependent on Nature. We can therefore say this: Nature produces Man out of itself; Man cannot be outside of Nature, he still has his being rooted in Nature. Therefore there cannot be any hostility between them. On the contrary, there must always be a friendly understanding between Man and Nature. Man came from Nature in order to see Nature in himself; that is, Nature came to itself in order to see itself in Man.

This is objective thinking, to say that Man comes from Nature and that Man sees himself through Nature, or that Nature sees itself through Man. There is another way of seeing into the situation, by shifting our position from objectivity to subjectivity. This probing into subjectivity is probing into the very basis of Nature as it is in itself.

To turn to subjectivity means to turn from Nature to Man himself. Instead of considering Man objectively in opposition to Nature, our task is now to make Man retreat, as it were, into himself and see what he finds in the depths of his being. The probing of Nature thus becomes the problem of Man: Who or what is Man?

.        .        .        .

A Zen master once asked a monk: "Do not think of good, do not think of evil; when no thoughts arise let me see your primary face."

The monk answered: "I have nothing shapely to show you."[1]

This kind of *mondo* ("question and answer") has taken place in Zen from its start in the T'ang period—that is, in the eighth century. To those who have never been initiated into the Zen way of treating the problem of Nature or Man this "question and answer" will appear uncouth and not susceptible of rationalization. It is altogether out of the realm of discursive understanding.

"What does 'the primary face' mean?", you may ask. What has "the face" to do with the problem of Man and his situation? And then what has one to do with good and evil and "no thoughts rising"? A few words may be needed before we can come to Zen.

Generally speaking, Zen refuses to make use of abstract terms, to indulge in metaphysical speculations, or to involve itself in a series of questions and answers. Its discourse is always short, pithy, and right to the point. When words are found to be a round-about way of communication, the Zen master may utter "Katz!" without giving what is ordinarily considered a rational or an intelligible reply.

In the same way, when told that he looks like a dog, he will not get excited and make an angry retort. Instead, he may simply cry "Bow-wow", and pass on!

As to the use of a stick, there is one master noted for its liberal application. Tokusan (Teh-shan, 790–865) used to say: "When you say 'Yes', you get thirty blows of my stick; when you say 'No', you get thirty blows of my stick just the same." The Zen monks generally carry a long staff in travelling from one monastery to another along the mountain path. The stick in Zen has been a very expressive means of communication. Zen thus avoids as much as possible the use of a medium, especially intellectual and conceptual, known as "language".

[1] *The Transmission of the Lamp* (*Dentoroku*), Fas. VIII, under "Nansen".

In the above cited *mondo*, therefore, we have first of all a reference to good and evil. This has nothing to do with our sense of moral evaluation, and simply refers to our dualistic habit of thinking. "Good and evil" can be anything: black and white, yes and no, affirmation and negation, creator and the created, heaven and hell, etc. When we are told not to think of them, it means to transcend all forms of dichotomy and to enter into the realm of the absolute where "no thought" prevails. The question, therefore, proposed by the Zen master here concerns the absolute and is not one of morality or psychology.

What does Zen mean by asking a man to show his "primary face"? When I tell you that this is the innermost man or self in itself or Being-as-it-is, you will be surprised and declare: "What an odd language Zen people use!" But this oddity partly characterizes the Chinese language as well as Zen.

"The primary face" is possessed by every one of us. According to Zen, it is not only physical but at once physical and metaphysical, material and spiritual, gross and subtle, concrete and abstract. The Zen master wants to see this kind of "face" presented to him by his monk. In one important sense "this face" must go through the baptism of "Do not think of good, do not think of evil", and of "Have no thoughts whatever". For the face we have on the surface of our relative psychological way of thinking is not "the primary face" demanded by the master.

But here is another difficulty, the answer given by the monk: "I have nothing shapely to show you." This means: "I am sorry, master, that my primary face is not very presentable, and not worthy of your regard." The monk seems to be talking about his own face, which is recognizable by every Tom, Dick, and Harry. Is this face really the "primary face"? If so, Zen does not seem to have anything miraculous about it. What, then, is all this fuss about going beyond the duality of our thinking? The Zen master's answer to such questions will be: "This is on the plane of pure subjectivity and a matter of personal determination." In fact all Zen *mondo* come out of this subjectivity experience.

Here is another *mondo*.

Monk: "Before my parents gave birth to me, where is my nose [or face or self]?"

Master: "When you are already born of your parents, where are you?"[1]

Here the monk has "the nose" instead of "the face", but this does not mean any difference as far as Zen is concerned. The Chinese masters always prefer to be concrete. Instead of talking about "Being" or "Reason" or "Reality", they talk about stones, flowers, clouds, or birds.

To give another example, when a Zen master was walking with his monk attendant he happened to notice a bird flying, and asked the monk: "What bird is that?" The monk answered: "It is gone already." The master turned toward the monk and taking hold of his nose gave it a twist. The monk cried in pain: "Oh! Oh!" The master remarked: "It is still there!" We notice here, too, the nose is playing an important role in the discussion of Being. No high-flown abstract terminology here, but ordinary plain talking on the plane of our daily experience. "The primary face", the painful "nose", the flying "bird", and, in fact, any sensuous object that is seen or heard turns into the subject of the deepest metaphysical significance in the hands of the Zen masters.

We have been digressing. In the *mondo* prior to the one just cited in regard to the flying bird, the monk wants to know where his nose is before he was born of his parents, or even before this earth or Nature came into being. This exactly corresponds to Christ's statement: "Before Abraham was, I am."[2] The "nose" is Christ and the monk is desirous of interviewing Christ himself who *is*, even before the birth of Abraham. Western people will never dare to ask such questions. They would think it sacrilegious to intrude on ground which is sacrosanct to

[1] *The Transmission of the Lamp*, Fas. VIII.  [2] John viii, 58.

all Christians or "God-fearing" minds. They are too dualistically minded and unable to think of going beyond tradition and history.

The master's answer is also significant. He ignores time-sequence in which birth-and-death takes place with all other events which make up human history. He pays no attention to the serialism of time. When the monk asks about his "nose" before his coming into this world of sense and intellect, the master retorts by referring to the monk's actual presence, to his "as-he-is-ness". From the relative point of view this answer is no answer; it does not locate the monk's "nose", but asks the counter-question regarding himself as he stands before the master, perhaps in a shabby monkish robe and with a not very smoothly shaven face and a not very shapely nose.

The point that I am trying to make is that Zen starts where time has not come to itself; that is to say, where timelessness has not negated itself so as to have a dichotomy of subject-object, Man-Nature, God-world. This is the abode of what I call "pure subjectivity". Zen is here and wants us to be here too. In terms of Nature, Zen is where one of the masters remarked: "When I began to study Zen, mountains were mountains; when I thought I understood Zen, mountains were not mountains; but when I came to full knowledge of Zen, mountains were again mountains."

When the mountains are seen as not standing against me, when they are dissolved into the oneness of things, they are not mountains, they cease to exist as objects of Nature. When they are seen as standing against me, as separate from me, as something unfriendly to me, they are not mountains either. The mountains are really mountains when they are assimilated into my being and I am absorbed in them. As long as Nature is something differentiated from me and is displayed before me as if it were an unknown quantity and a mere brute fact, Nature cannot be said even to be unfriendly or actively hostile.

On the other hand, Nature becomes part of my being

as soon as it is recognized as Nature, as *pour-soi*. It can never remain as something strange and altogether unrelated to me. I am in Nature and Nature is in me. Not mere participation in each other, but a fundamental identity between the two. Hence, the mountains are mountains and the rivers are rivers; they are there before me. The reason I can see the mountains as mountains and the waters as waters is because I am in them and they are in me; that is, *tat tvam asi*. If not for this identity, there would be no Nature as *pour-soi*. "The primary face" or "my nose" is to be taken hold of here and nowhere else.

Identity belongs in spatial terminology. In terms of time, it is timelessness. But mere timelessness does not mean anything. When Nature is seen as confronting me there is already time, and timelessness now turns itself into time. But time-serialism makes sense only when it goes on in the field of timelessness, which is the Buddhist conception of *sunyata* ("emptiness"). In this *sunyata* the mountains are mountains and I see them as such and they see me as such; my seeing them is their seeing me. It is then that *sunyata* becomes *tathata* ("suchness"); *tathata* is *sunyata* and *sunyata* is *tathata*.

When we come to this stage of thinking, pure subjectivity is pure objectivity, the *en-soi* is the *pour-soi*; there is perfect identity of Man and Nature, of God and Nature, of the one and the many. But the identity does not imply the annihilation of one at the cost of the other. The mountains do not vanish; they stand before me. I have not absorbed them, nor have they wiped me out of the scene. The dichotomy is there, which is suchness, and this suchness (*tathata*) in all its suchness is emptiness (*sunyata*) itself. The mountains are mountains and yet not mountains. I am I and you are you, and yet I am you and you are I. Nature as a world of manyness is not ignored, and Man as a subject facing the many remains conscious of himself.

6

Zen avoids discoursing or arguing, for this leads us nowhere after much ado. Zen does not make light of philosophy and of all that drives us to philosophizing, but Zen's business is to make us realize that philosophizing does not exhaust the human urge to reach the ultimate. Hence the following *mondo*:

Yakusan (Yueh-shan Wei-yen, 750–834) asked Ungan (Yun-yen T'an-ch'eng, 781–841): "I understand you know how to play with the lion. Am I correct?"

Ungan: "Yes, you are right."

Yakusan: "How many lions can you play with?"

Ungan: "Six."

Yakusan: "I also know how to play with the lion."

Ungan: "How many?"

Yakusan: "Just one."

Ungan: "One is six and six is one."[1]

Ungan later came to Isan (Kwei-shan Ling-yu, 771–853) and Isan asked: "I am told that you knew how to play with the lion when you were at the Yakusan monastery. Is that right?"

Ungan said: "That is right."

Isan went on: "Do you play with it all the time? Or do you sometimes give it a rest?"

Ungan: "If I wish to play with it, I play; if I wish to give it a rest, I give it a rest."

Isan: "When it is at rest, where is it?"

Ungan: "At rest, at rest!"[2]

The lion which is the subject of the *mondo* here is Nature and the player is the self or "subjectum", as I would sometimes call the self. Nature is held at five points (six according to Buddhist psychology) by the self. When Isan says that he knows how to play with six lions, he refers to our five (or six) senses wherewith Nature is taken hold of. The senses are like the windows through which

---

[1] *The Transmission of the Lamp*, Fas. XIV.
[2] Ibid.

Nature is observed. Nature may, for all we know, be more than that, but we have no more than the five senses, beyond which we have no means to differentiate Nature. In a physical world of senses more than five (or six) we should perceive something more in Nature, and our life would be richer to that extent. Seven windows would surely give us more of Nature. This is, however, a mere possibility worked out by looking through the sense-windows as we have them, which are aided by the intellect or the *mano-vijnana*, according to Buddhist psychology. From this, we can think of a world of four or more dimensions, indeed of any number. Mathematicians have all kinds of numbers, imaginary, negative, complex, etc., which are of no sensuous demonstration. Our actual physical world is limited. We can think of an infinitely extending space, but specialists tell us that space is limited and that it is mathematically calculable.

What concerns Zen is the problem of the self which plays with the "six lions" or looks out through the "six windows"—the subjectum, or what I call pure subjectivity. This is what interests Zen and Zen wants us to get acquainted with it. But the Zen way of acquaintance is unique, for it does not proceed with the dichotomy of Man-Nature or subject-object. Zen takes us at once to the realm of non-dichotomy, which is the beginningless beginning of all things. Time has not yet come to its own consciousness. Zen is where this consciousness is about to rise. Or it may be better to say that consciousness is caught at the very moment of rising from the unconscious. This moment is an absolute present, the crossing point of time and timelessness, of the conscious and unconscious. This crossing moment, which is the rising moment of an *ekacittakshana*, that is, the moment of no-mind or no-thought, refuses to be expressed in language, in words of the mouth. It is a matter of personal determination.

While Ungan was sweeping the ground, Isan asked: "You are busily employed, are you not?"

Ungan: "There is one who is not at all busily employed."

Isan: "In that case you mean to say that there is a second moon?"

Ungan set up the broom and said: "What number is this moon?"

Isan nodded and went away.

Gensha (Hsuan-sha Shih-pei, 834–908), hearing of this, remarked: "This is no other than a second moon!"[1]

"A second moon" refers to a dualistic conception of the self. There is one who is busily engaged in work and there is another who is not working and quietly unmoved observes all that goes before him. This way of thinking is not Zen. In Zen there is no such separation between worker and observer, movement and mover, seer and the seen, subject and object. In the case of Ungan, the sweeping and the sweeper and the broom are all one, even including the ground which is being swept. There is no second moon, no third moon, no first moon either. This is beyond verbalism. But Man is no Man unless he knows how to communicate. Hence Ungan's setting up the broom. The language of Zen has characteristics of its own.

To give another example: When Ungan was making tea, Dogo (Tao-wu Yuan-chih, 779–835) came in and asked: "To whom are you serving tea?"

Ungan: "There is one who wants it."

Dogo: "Why don't you make him serve himself?"

Ungan: "Fortunately, I am here."[2]

"I" is the one who wants tea and also the one who makes tea; "I" is the server and the served.

Ungan once asked a nun: "Is your father still alive?"

The nun answered: "Yes, master."

Ungan: "How old is he?"

Nun: "Eighty."

Ungan: "You have a father whose age is not eighty, do you know him?"

Nun: "Is he not the one who thus comes?"

Ungan: "He is still a child [of his]."[3]

The problem of the self evaporates into sheer ab-

[1] *The Transmission of the Lamp,* Fas. XIV.    [2] Ibid.    [3] Ibid.

straction when pursued analytically, leaving nothing behind. Zen realizes this; hence Ungan's setting up the broom, which is an eloquent demonstration. When appeal is made to verbalism, which takes place frequently, such references to "father" or to "I" point out where the Zen way of thinking tends as to the use of words.

## 7

Pure subjectivity, as sometimes supposed, is not to be located where "not one *cittakshana* ('thought-instant' or *nien* or *nen*) has yet been awakened". This is condemned by Zen masters as "nonsensical" or "useless". Nor is pure subjectivity pure timelessness, for it works in time and is time. It is not Man facing Nature as an unfriendly stranger but Man thoroughly merged in Nature, coming out of Nature and going into Nature, and yet conscious of himself as distinguishable in a unique way. But their distinguishability is not conceptual, and can be prehended as such in what I call *prajna*-intuition in timeless time, in an absolute present.

Daido of Tosu (Ta-tung of T'ou-tzu-shan, 819–914) was asked: "Who is Vairocana-Buddha?"[1]

Tosu answered: "He already has a name."

"Who is the master of Vairocana-Buddha?"

"Prehend (*hui-ch'u*) him when Vairocana has not yet come to existence."

The highest being is to be comprehended or intuited even prior to time. It is the Godhead who *is*, even before it became God and created the world. The Godhead is the one in whom there was yet neither Man nor Nature. "The master of Vairocana" is the Godhead. When he came to have "a name", he is no more the Master. To have "a name" for Vairocana is to make him negate himself. The Godhead negates himself by becoming God,

---

[1] *The Transmission of the Lamp*, Fas. XV. This may be regarded as corresponding to the Christian God, though not as creator.

the creator, for he then has "a name". In the beginning there is "the word", but in the beginningless beginning there is the Godhead who is nameless and no-word.

Zen calls this "mind of no-mind", "the unconscious conscious", "original enlightenment", "the originally pure", and very frequently just "this" (che-ko). But as soon as a name is given the Godhead ceases to be Godhead, Man and Nature spring up and we are caught in the maze of an abstract, conceptual vocabulary. Zen avoids all this, as we have seen. Some may say that Zen is rich in suggestions but that philosophy needs more, that we must go further into the field of analysis and speculation and verbalization. But the truth is that Zen never suggests; it directly points at "this", or produces "this" before you in order that you may see it for yourself. It is then for you to build up your own philosophical system to your intellectual satisfaction, for Zen does not despise intellection merely as such.

In point of fact Zen constantly uses words against its own declaration that it stands outside all words. So long as Zen is of Man while yet not of Man it cannot help it. Take up the following *mondo* and see how Zen makes use of words, and communicates what cannot be communicated.

A monk asked a master: "I am told that even when the sky is devoid of clouds it is not the original sky. What is the original sky, O master?"

The master said: "It is a fine day today for airing the wheat, young man."[1]

This is no answer from the relative point of view. For when we are asked such questions we generally try to define "the original sky" itself. The master mentions wheat because they lived very close to the field and were much dependent on the harvests. The wheat might easily be rice or hay. And if the master felt at the time like taking a walk, he might have said: "Let us saunter out for relaxation. We have lately been confined too much to the study."

[1] *Transmission of the Lamp*, Fas. XIV, under "Dogo".

On another occasion, the master was more education-
ally disposed and appealed to the following method. One
day, Sekiso (Ch'ing-chu of Shih-shuang shan, 807–888),
one of his chief disciples, asked: "When you pass away,
O master, how should I answer if people come and ask
me about the deepest secrets of reality?"

The master, Dogo, called to his boy attendant, who
answered: "Yes, master." Dogo told him to fill the pitcher
with clean water, and remained silent for a little while. He
then asked Sekiso: "What did you ask me about just
now?" Sekiso naturally repeated the question. But the
master apparently paid no attention to his disciple and
left the room.

Was this not a most curious way of treating a most
fundamental question of life? Sekiso was serious, but the
master treated him as if he were not concerned with the
question or the questioner. From our usual way of thinking, Dogo was highly enigmatic in his behaviour and
bizarre in his pedagogic methodology. What should we
make of him and his way of handling Zen?

This "calling and responding" (hu-ying) is one of the
methods frequently used by Zen masters in order to make
us come to a Zen awakening. The awakening itself is a
simple psychological event, but its significance goes deep
down to the basic make-up of human and cosmic consciousness. For we humans thereby penetrate into the
structure of reality which is behind the dichotomy of
subject and object, of Man and Nature, of God and Man.
In terms of time we are back at the point where there is
yet no consciousness or mind or intellectualization; therefore, it is a moment of timelessness, a moment of no-ekacit-
takshana rising in the breast of the Godhead. A satori-
event takes place at this moment, and there is for the first
time a possibility of communication—a wonderful event,
biologically speaking, in the evolution of consciousness, in
which Nature comes to itself and becomes Man, known in
Zen as "the original face" or "the nose" or "the primary
man". In fact various other concrete names are given to
"Man". This, however, is not symbolization.

There is a story told of a great Chinese Buddhist thinker called Dosho (Tao-sheng, died 434) who, when he found his intuition not acceptable to his contemporaries, talked to rocks in the desert. Before the introduction in China of a complete text of the *Mahaparinirvana Sutra*, scholars were in doubt as to the possibility of the Buddha-nature being present in all beings regardless of their sentiency or consciousness. But the philosopher in question was convinced that every being, man or no-man, was in possession of the Buddha-nature. Later, when a complete *Nirvana Sutra* was translated into Chinese, this was found to have been actually told by Buddha. In the meantime the philosopher was expelled as a heretic from the Buddhist community of the time. But being absolutely sure of his intuition, he is said to have discoursed on the topic to a mass of rocks in the field. They were found to be nodding, showing that they were in perfect agreement with the speaker.

The allusion in the following *mondo* to the rocks is based on this incident, recorded in the history of Chinese Buddhism during the period of Six Dynasties (317–589 A.D.).

Ungan once asked a monk: "Where have you been?"

The monk answered: "We have been talking together on the rock."

The master asked: "Did the rock nod, or not?"

The monk did not reply, whereupon the master remarked: "The rock had been nodding even before you began to talk."

In the case of Dosho, the rocks nodded in response to his talk on the omnipresence of the Buddha-nature, but in this *mondo* Ungan remarks that the rock had been nodding even prior to Dosho's eloquent discourse. Nature is already Man, or otherwise no Man could come out of it. It is ourselves who fail to be conscious of the fact.

8

Hiju Yesho (P'ai-shu Hui-hsing), a disciple of Yueh-shan Wei-yen, was asked by a monk: "What is Buddha?"

Yesho answered: "The cat is climbing up the post."

The monk confessed his inability to understand the master.

The latter said: "You ask the post."[1]

To those who for the first time come across such a *mondo* as this, the Zen master will appear as one who has lost his head. In the first place, what has Buddha to do with the cat, the post, and her climbing it? And then how can the post explain to the monk what the master means by these strange references?

However far we go with our usual reasoning, we cannot make anything out of this *mondo*. Either we are out of our human faculties or the master is moving somewhere where our customary walk does not take us. No doubt, there is a realm of transcendence where all the Zen masters have their exclusive abode, and Nature must be hiding this from our world of sense-and-intellect.

Juten (Pao-fu Ts'ung-chan, died 928),[2] seeing a monk come to him, struck the post with his staff and then struck the monk. The monk felt the pain and exclaimed: "It hurts!" The master remarked: "How is it that 'that' does not cry out in pain?"

The monk failed to answer.

Here is another reference to the post. The post is an object in Nature. As long as it stands against Man, it is unintelligent and shows in it no sign of friendliness. But let Man see it or hear it, and it immediately becomes a part of Man and feels him in every ingredient of its being. It will surely nod its head when Man questions it. Therefore, when a master heard a monk striking the board in front of the Meditation Hall, it is said that he cried: "It hurts!"

This is the reason why Zen masters are frequently approached with the question: "What is your 'environment' (*kyogai*)?" The reference is to Nature, and the question is to find out how it affects them, or, more exactly, how the masters inwardly respond to Nature. Even this does not quite accurately interpret what the term "*kyogai*" (here

[1] *The Transmission of the Lamp*, Fas. XIV.　　[2] Op. cit., 19.

rendered as "environment") signifies. It may not be out of place to say a few words in regard to this term, for it has a weighty bearing on our understanding Zen in its relation to Nature.

I do not think there is any English word which truly corresponds to this Chinese and Japanese word. *Kyogai* (*ching-ai*) originally comes from the Sanskrit *gocara* or *vishaya* or *gati*, which mean more or less the same thing. They are a "realm" or "field" where any action may take place. *Gocara* is especially significant; it means "the pasture" where cows graze and walk about. As the cattle have their grazing field, man has a field or realm for his inner life. The wise man has his *Weltanschauung* whereby he views the whole world, and this enters into the content of his *kyogai*. The *kyogai* is his mode or frame or tone of consciousness from which all his reactions come and wherein all outside stimulations are absorbed. We generally imagine that we all live in the same objective world and behave in the same way. But the truth is that none of us has the same *kyogai*. For each of us lives in his inner sanctum, which is his subjectivity and which cannot be shared by any other individual. This strictly individual inner structure or frame of consciousness, utterly unique, is one's *kyogai*. When a monk asks a master what his *kyogai* is, the monk wishes to know his inner life, his "spiritual" environment. The question, therefore, is equivalent to asking what is one's Zen understanding. And it goes without saying that this Zen understanding is Zen's response to Nature, including Nature's role in Zen.

From the several *mondo* already quoted, we can see that the masters are totally identified with Nature. To them there is no distinction between the *en-soi* and the *pour-soi*, nor is there any attempt on their part to identify themselves with Nature or to make Nature participate in their life. The masters simply express themselves at the point where time has not yet cut, as it were, into timelessness. It may be, however, better to say that they are at the crossing or cutting point itself and that it is this point that makes the masters the instruments of communication in order that Nature may become conscious of itself. Pure Being descends from its seat of absolute identity and, becoming dichotomous, speaks to itself. This is what Zen calls the master's *kyogai* or his "frame of consciousness", or his inner life, which is his Zen way of behaving.

Let me quote a few more examples in which the masters make constant reference to Nature as if the latter were other than themselves. Here are some of the answers the masters gave to their inquisitive monks:[1]

1. "The full moon in the autumnal sky shines on the ten thousand houses."

2. "The mountains and rivers, in full extension, lie before you, and there is nothing to hinder your surveying glance."

3. "The white clouds are rising as far as one's eyes can survey from every peak of the mountain range; while a fine drizzling rain falls silently outside the bamboo screens."

4. "The green bamboos are swaying in the winds; the cold pine trees are shivering in the moonlight."

5. When a monk asked if anything of Buddhism could be formed in the desert, the master answered: "The larger rocks and the smaller rocks."

6. A master took a monk, who was eager to know the secrets of Zen teaching, into a bamboo grove and told the monk: "You see that some of these bamboos are crooked while others are growing up straight."

7. When a master wanted to tell a monk what the mind of Buddha was, he said: "The white cow is lying by the cool stream in the open field."

8. When a Confucian scholar visited a Zen master, he asked: "What is the ultimate secret of Zen?" The master answered: "You have a fine saying in your *Analects*: 'I have nothing to hide from you.' So has Zen nothing hidden from you."

"I cannot understand," said the scholar.

Later, they had a walk together along the mountain

[1] The following are culled haphazard from *The Transmission of the Lamp*.

path. The wild laurel happened to be blooming. The master said: "Do you smell the fragrance of the flowering tree?" The scholar responded: "Yes, I do." "Then," declared the master, "I have hidden nothing from you."

9. A monk was anxious to learn Zen and said: "I have been newly initiated into the Brotherhood. Will you be gracious enough to show me the way to Zen? The master said: "Do you hear the murmuring sound of the mountain stream?" The monk answered: "Yes, I do." The master said: "Here is the entrance."

10. To a monk's question about the ultimate meaning of Buddhism, a master answered: "A stream of water is flowing out of the mountains, and there are no obstacles that would ever stop its course." Then he added:

"The mountain-flowers are spread out like gold brocades. Here is Manjusri striking right into your eyes.

"The birds in the secluded depths of the woodland are singing their melodies each in their own way. Here is Avalokiteshvara filling up your ears.

"O monk! What is there that makes you go on reflecting and cogitating?"

11. A master once gave the following verse in appreciation of his relationship to his mountain retreat:

"Peak over peak of mountains endlessly above the bridge;
One long stream below the bridge flowing on mile after mile;
There is one lonely white heron
That is my constant visitor at this retreat."

## 9

These quotations from *The Transmission of the Lamp*, which is a store-house of Zen *mondo*, Zen stories, and Zen sermons, abundantly illustrate the relationship in which Zen stands to Nature and the role which Nature plays in the make-up of Zen. Indeed, Zen cannot be separated

from Nature, for Zen knows no polarization. Pure subjectivity from which Zen starts absorbs all that constitutes
Nature or the objective world so called.

Karl Jaspers distinguishes three realms of Being:
Being-there, Being-oneself, and Being-in-itself, and then
proceeds to state that these three realms "are in no sense
reducible to one another". Blackham in his *Six Existen-
tialist Thinkers* (p. 58) speaks for Jaspers:

"The person who is made aware of them may participate
in all three; Transcendence embraces the world of objects and
subjects: but the logical understanding, founded upon the
objects of empirical existence, being-there, is unable without
falsification to describe the other realms of existence or to
bring them into a common system; their discontinuity is
invincible, only to be reconciled in the *life* of a person and *by
faith* in Transcendence."[1]

Now, the ways of the philosopher are to talk about a
"system", "continuity", "reconciliation", "logical understanding", etc. But the philosopher starts with "logicism"
and then tries to come to "life" instead of reversing the
process. In "life" itself there is no reconciling, no systema-
tizing, no understanding; we just live it and all is well
with us. "To awaken philosophic faith in Transcendence"
is also unnecessary, for this is something added to life by
the so-called logical understanding. Nor is there in life
itself any such distinction as the "three realms of being".
All these things are piling so many heads over the one
which is there from the very first. The original one is
buried deeper and deeper as we go on philosophizing, and
finally we lose sight of it.

Seppo (Hsueh-feng I-ts'un, 822–908) once gave this
sermon to his monks: "You are all like those who, while
immersed in the ocean, extend their hands crying for
water." This is really the human situation in which we
who call ourselves rational and thinking find ourselves.

But human life is not like that of other living beings.

[1] The italics are mine.

We do not want to live just an animal life; we like to know the worth of life and to appreciate it consciously. This is, however, the very moment wherein we negate ourselves by deviating from life itself. It is for this reason that we philosophize and become "thinkers". But it is not by thinking that we come back to life, nor is it by "philosophic faith" or by "divine revelation" that we are brought to the presence and the silence of "Transcendence". Zen, however, does not like the odour of abstraction which oozes out from even such terms as "Transcendence". For, in fact, as soon as appeal is made to words, we leave life itself and involve ourselves in every kind of "logical" controversy. We construct our own traps and then struggle to escape from them, and as long as we are what we are, we cannot get away from this dilemma. It is only for those who have attained *prajna*-intuition that an escape is provided from the almost hopeless intricacies of intellection.

In the meantime, every one of us feels an inward urge to effect such an escape in one way or another. The philosophic way is to appeal to Reason, in whatever sense the term may be interpreted, whereas the "religiously" inclined resort to "faith" or "revelation". The Zen way of escape—or, better, of solution—is direct apprehension or grasping "it" or "this".

"This" is pure subjectivity, or being-in-itself, or absolute self. It is also called "the one passage to the highest" or "the one solitary way of escape". There are many names given to this way of Zen, for almost every master had his own terminology. In spite of these endless complexities, all Zen masters strive to express that something in our life as we live it which gives us the key to the difficulties raised by the intellect and also stills the anxieties produced by our attachment to a world of relativities.

We can have a glimpse into this truth in a few extracts from Zen masters' discourses on the use of words:

1. Question: "Whenever appeal is made to words, there is a taint. What is the truth of the highest order (*hiang-shang shih*)?"

Answer: "Whenever appeal is made to words, there is a taint."

2. Question: "Where is one solitary road to being oneself?"[1]

Answer: "Why trouble yourself to ask about it?"

3. Question: "Fine words and wonderful meanings make up the contents of the Doctrine. Can you show me a direct way without resorting to a triple treatment?"

Answer: "Fare thee well."[2]

4. Question: "Whenever appeal is made to words, we are sure to fall into every form of snare. Please, O master, tell me how to deal directly with it."

Answer: "You come to me after doing away with every kind of measuring instrument."[3]

I should like to add a few words here on escapism, with which some writers on Buddhism try to connect Zen.

"To escape", or "to be emancipated", or "to be disengaged", or any word or phrase implying the idea of keeping oneself away from a world of becoming, is altogether inadequate to express the Zen way of achieving "salvation". Even "salvation" is a bad term, because Zen recognizes nothing from which we are to be saved. We are from the first already "saved" in all reality, and it is due to our ignorance of the fact that we talk about being saved or delivered or freed. So with "escape", etc., Zen knows no traps or complexities from which we are to escape. The traps or complexities are our own creation. We find ourselves, and when we realize this, we are what we have been from the very beginning of things.

For example, we create the three realms, to use Jaspers' terms, of "being-there", "being-oneself", and "being-in-itself"; or the two modes according to Sartre of *en-soi* and *pour-soi*, or the two categories in Western thinking of God and the created, or of God and Nature, or of Man and Nature. These are all of human creation, and we cling to

[1] Or "transcendence", or "escape".
[2] Or, "Take good care of yourself."
[3] All these four *mondo* are quoted from *The Transmission of the Lamp*, Fas. XVIII.

them as if they were absolutely determined, binding us as something inextricably, fatalistically unescapable. We are our own prisoners. We defeat ourselves, believing in defeatism, which is itself our own creation. This is our ignorance, known as *avidya* in Buddhism. When this is recognized we realize that we are free, "men of no-business" (*Wu-shih chih jen*).

Zen, therefore, does not try to disengage us from the world, to make us mere spectators of the hurly-burly which we see around us. Zen is not mysticism, if the latter is to be understood in the sense of escapism. Zen is right in the midst of the ocean of becoming. It shows no desire to escape from its tossing waves. It does not antagonize Nature; it does not treat Nature as if it were an enemy to be conquered, nor does it stand away from Nature. It is indeed Nature itself.

Buddhism is often regarded as pessimistic and as urging us to escape from the bondage of birth and death. Dr. Rhys Davids, for instance, states that "the ultimate goal of Buddhism is to untie the knots of Existence and find a way to escape".[1] This way of interpreting Buddhism has been going on among Buddhist scholars as well as Buddhist devotees, but it is not in conformity with the spirit of Buddha as one who experienced Enlightenment and declared himself as the all-conqueror, the all-knower, the all-seer.

10

We have now come to the point where our discourse on "pure subjectivity" finally leads us. For "pure subjectivity" is no other than "pure objectivity". Our inner life is complete when it merges into Nature and becomes one with it. There is nothing, after all, in the Zen master's *kyogai* (*gocara, ching-ai*), which differentiates itself as something wondrous or extraordinary. It consists, as in all other cases, in scenting the fragrance of the laurel in

---

[1] Quoted by H. S. Wadia in *The Message of Buddha*, p. 170, London, J. M. Dent, 1938.

bloom and in listening to a bird singing on a spring day
to its heart's content. What, however, makes a difference
in the case of a Zen master is that he sees the flowers as
they really are and not in a dreamy sort of way in which
the flowers are not real flowers and the rivers are not
really flowing rivers. Pure subjectivity, instead of vapor-
izing realities, as one might imagine, consolidates everything with which it comes in touch. More than that, it
gives a soul to even non-sentient beings and makes them
readily react to human approach. The whole universe
which means Nature ceases to be "hostile" to us as we
had hitherto regarded it from our selfish point of view.
Nature, indeed, is no more something to be conquered
and subdued. It is the bosom whence we come and
whither we go.

There is, then, in the teaching of Zen no escapism, no
mysticism, no denial of existence, no conquering Nature,
no frustrations, no mere utopianism, no naturalism. Here
is a world of the given. Becoming is going on in all its
infinitely varied forms, and yet there is the realm of
transcendence within all these changing scenes. Emptiness
is Suchness and Suchness is Emptiness. A world of *rupa*
is no other than *sunyata*, and *sunyata* is no other than this
*rupaloka*, which is a Buddhist term for Nature.

Dokai of Fuyo (Fu-jung Tao-k'ai, died 1118),[1] of the
Sung dynasty, writes in one of his poems on the relationship between Emptiness and Suchness:

> From the very first, not one dharma[2] is in existence; all
>     is Emptiness;
> And where in this is there room for talk about being
>     enlightened in the Perfect Way?
> Thus I thought no intelligence has ever come to us from
>     the Shorin,[3]
> But, lo! the peach blossoms as of old are smiling in the
>     spring breeze.

[1] Supplementary volumes to *The Transmission of the Lamp*, Fas. X.
[2] A thing, an object, that which subsists.
[3] The Shorin (Shao-lin) is the temple where Bodhi-Dharma is said to
have retreated after his unsuccessful interview with Wu, the Emperor of the
Liang, and spent nine years absorbed in meditation.

Seccho (Hsueh-tou), of the eleventh century, has the following stanza in which he finds himself musing surrounded by the trees and looking at the stream filled with the illusive shadows of the mountains. Is he musing? Is he lost in a dream? What philosophy has he here?

> The spring mountains are covered with greens, layer after layer, in utter confusion;
> The shadows are seen serenely reflected in the spring waters below.
> Between the heavens and the earth in a lonely field
> I stand all by myself before a vista whose end nobody knows.[1]

We must now come to the conclusion. I have not so far been able to be even tentatively complete in my treatment of the subject. There are many other matters left out, among which I would mention the problem of necessity and freedom. We think Nature is brute fact, entirely governed by the laws of absolute necessity; and there is no room for freedom to enter here. But Zen would say that Nature's necessity and Man's freedom are not such divergent ideas as we imagine, but that necessity is freedom and freedom is necessity.

A second important problem in Zen's treatment of Nature is that of teleology. Has Zen any purposefulness when it declares that the sun rises in the morning and that I eat when hungry? To discuss the matter fully requires time and space, more than we can afford at this session.

A third problem is that of good and evil. What has Zen to say about morality? What relationship is there between Zen and the Western idea of the divine commands which imply fear and obedience? To this Zen would say that Zen is on the other shore of good and evil, but this does not mean that Zen is unconcerned with ethics.

A fourth problem is the fact of human depravity. In other words, what has Zen to say about demonology?

[1] *The Hekigah Shu (Pi-yen Chi).*

Nature has no demons; they are human creations. It is Man who peoples Nature with all kinds of demons and permits them to do him all kinds of evil. It is an interesting subject, especially seeing that Man with all his boast of his rationality keeps on committing deeds of irrationality —that is, of demonology.

# INDEX

(C = Chinese, J = Japanese, S = Sanskrit)

ABSOLUTE, see 'Originally Pure'
Absolute present, 190, 192
*Acintya* ('unthinkable,' S), 91
Affirmation and negation, 90
Ananda, 12
Approximation, stage of, 76
Asceticism, Zen not, 28
*Avatamsaka Sutra,* see Kegon
*Avidya* ('nescience,' S), 203

BASIS of religious experience, 141 n.
Baso (Ma-tsu C) (*d.* 788), 57, 80, 131, 139 f., 159
Being, according to Jaspers, 200
Being and non-being, 62, 71 ff.
Benefits of *dhyana* according to *Candra-dipa-samadhi Sutra,* 41 f.
Birth-and-death, 51; Hui-neng on, 32
Blows with staff, 25
*Bodhi* ('Enlightenment,' S), 32, 137
Bodhidharma (Daruma, J; Ta-mo, C) (*d.* 528), 28th Indian and 1st Chinese Zen Patriarch, 13, 14, 15, 22 f., 44
'Bodhidharma's coming from the West,' significance of, 58, 80 ff., 143
'*Bodhisattva* of No-miracles,' 150 f.
*Bodhi*-tree, stanzas on, 16 f.
Bones, Bodhidharma's, 23
Bridge, flowing, 86, 125
'Buddha, who is the?', 113 f.
'Buddha a murderer,' 132, 158
Buddha-Heart, Sect of (= Zen), 11
Buddha-image, Tanka's burning of, 127 f.
Buddha-nature in all things, 195; Yikwan on, 91
Bunsui on the Self, 110
*Bushido,* see Samurai

'CALLING and responding,' see *hu-ying*
*Candradipa-samadhi Sutra,* 41
Categories self-created, 202 f.
Causation and Zen, 152 f.
Celibacy, 155
Cesspool, Buddha like, according to Rinzai, 23
Ch'an (C = Ben), 11
'Ch'an of the mouth-corners,' 132
*Chih* (C=*prajna*-intuition), 139 f., 144 f., 150 f.
Chih-i (Chigi, J) (538-597), Buddhist philosopher, 139, 155; see also Tendai
Chinese character and Zen, 33 f., 155 f.
*Ching-ai,* see 'environment'
*Ching-teh Chuan-teng Lu* (C), see *Transmission of the Lamp*
Ch'ing-yuan, see Seigen
Christ, 186
Chu Hsi, 161 f.
Circle without circumference, 153
*Citta-ksana* ('thought-instant,' S), 190, 192; see *ekacittaksana*
Clinging, rejection of, 24
'Common mortals are Buddhas,' 32
Concepts abhorred by Zen, 48 f., 53 f.

Confucianism and Zen, 33, 34, 160 f.
'Conquest of nature,' Western ideal, 178 ff.
Contemplation is creation, 123
'Craziness' of Zen, 157 ff.
Creation is contemplation, 123

DAIAN, 62 f., 64 f.
Daido (Ta-tung (819-914), 175, 192
Daigu (Tai-yu), 26
Daishu Yekai, 44 f.
Dai-ten (Ta-tien), 148 f.
Daiye, 70 f.
Daizui (Tai-shui), 168 ff.
Daruma, see Bodhidharma
Demons human creations, 205 f.
*Dentoroku* (J), see *Transmission of the Lamp*
Dharma, see Bodhidharma
*Dharma* (S), meaning of word, 124
*Dharmas,* 85, 124, 204
*Dhyana* (S, here=Zen), 11, 37–42, 137, 162 f.; distinguished from original *dhyana* after Hui-neng, 162
*Dhyana* and Hinduism, 42–4
Dialectic, 169 ff.
*Dialogue of the Buddha and Mahapitaka Brahmaraja,* 12
*Diamond Sutra (Vajracchedika Sutra),* 86, 125; Tokusan and, 126
Direct insight, 42 f.
Dirt-scraper, 134
Discrimination, 51 f.
Dofuku (Tao-fu), disciple of Bodhid-harma, 22
Dogen, introduced Soto Zen to Japan (1233), 20
Dogo (Tao-wu) (779-835), 52 f., 148, 149, 150 f., 191, 194
Doiku (Tao-yu), disciple of Bodhid-harma, 23
Dokai of Fuyo, 204
Doshin (Toa-hsin), 4th Patriarch, 15, 138
Dosho (Tao-sheng, *d.* 434), 195; see also 118, n. 66, 128
Dragon, One-Eyed (Myosho), 63, 67 f.
Drum, Kwasan's, 76 f.
Dualism, 191
Dung, stick of, 134

*Eastern Buddhist, The,* 7
Echo as answer, 167
Eckhart, Meister (German mystic, *ca.* 1260-1327), 59, 75, 79, 153
*Ekacittaksana* ('one-thought-moment'), 190, 194
Emptiness, see *sunyata*
'Empty-handed I hold the spade,' 125
Enlightenment, see *bodhi*; *Essentials of Sudden,* 44 f.
'Environment' (*kyogai,* J; *ching-ai,* C), 196-8
Epistemology, Zen, 146
Escape, Zen way of, 201 f.

*Essentials of Sudden Enlightenment, On the (Tongo Yomon Ron*, J; *Tun-wu Yao-men Lun*, C), by Daishu Yekai, 44 f.
'Everyday thought the Tao,' Baso (Matsu) on, 139 f.
'Eye of the Dharma', 12

*Fa pao t'an ching* (or *Sutra of Wei Lang*), sermons of Hui-neng *(q.v.)*, 16, 29 ff., 47
'Face, original,' 18
Fa-tsang, Buddhist philosopher (*d.* 712), 139, 155; see also *Kegon*
Feudalism, Japanese, and Zen, 34—6
Fichte, J. G. (German philosopher, 1762—1814), 79
Flesh, Bodhidharma's, 23
Forty-volume *Kegon*, see *Gandavyuha*
Freedom, 202 f.
Fuke upsets dinner-table, 126

*Gandavyuha Sutra* (part of *Kegon*), 139; quoted 49 ff.
Ganto (Yen-tou) (829—887), 76
Gensha (Hsuan-sha) (834—908), 82—3, 191
Gensoku (Hsuan-tse), 96
*Gocara* ('pasture,' S = 'environment'), 197
God and Man, 178
Godhead, 149, 170 f., 192 f.; in mysticism, 75
'God of Fire,' 96
God's will, 166—7
Goso, 71, 73

HALO, 168 f.
Hearing, stage of, 76
*Heki-gan Shu (Pi-Yen Chi)*, Zen 'case-book' by Seccho and Yengo, 46, 205
Hiju Yesho, 195 f.
Historical approach to Zen inadequate, 135, 143 f.
*Ho*, see *kwatsu*
Hogen (Fa-yen), 95 f.
*Hsin* ('soul', C), 15
*Hsing-chiao* ('travelling on foot,' C), 134
Hsing-yen, see *Kyogen*
Huang-po, see Obaku
*Hua-yen*, see *Kegon*
Hui-k'o, see Shen-Kuang; see also Yeka
Hui-neng or Wei Lang (Yeno), 6th Zen Patriarch in China, 15, 17 ff., 29 ff., 44, 48, 97, 131, 136 f.
Hung-jen, 5th Patriarch in China 16 f.
Hu Shih, Dr., sometime President of National Peking University, 129 ff.
*Hu-ying* ('calling and responding' C), 194

*I chu* (C), see 'one word'
Identity doctrine (i.e. *dhyana=prajna*), 138 ff., 163
Immediacy not referring to time, 87 ff., 119 f., 126
Immediacy, Yakusan on reason for, 149 f.
Immortality, see being-and-non-being
'Inch's difference,' 96, 126
'Inside men,' 148 f.
Insignia not handed down by Hui-neng, 18 f.

Intellect not *chih*, 144
Intellectuality, 163
Intuition, 28, 54 f., 85 ff; see also *prajna*
Irrationality of nature, 181
Isan (=Reiyu?) (*d.* 853), and the nun Ryutetsuma, 77 f.
I-san (Kwei-shan Ling-yu) (771—834), 126, 161 f., 168 f., 190 f.

JASPERS, Karl, on being, 200
*Jen-yun*, 142 n.
*Jhana* (Pali=*Dhyana*), 11
Jinne, see Shen-hui
Jinshu (Shen-hsiu), 138
Jones, Rufus, 75
Joshu (Ch'ao-chou) (778—897), 168, 174 f.
Joye, 96, 97
'Just this and nothing more,' 142 f., 193
Juten, 112

KAITOTSU of Tozen, 110
Kamakura, 35
Kasyapa, see Mahakasyapa
*Kegon (Avatamsaka Sutra)*, 102, 116, 139
Keishin, 140
Keisho, 102 f.
*Keitoku Dento* (J), see *Transmission of the Lamp*
Ki of Unryu-in, 110
Knowledge, kinds of, 140, 144, 146
Knowledge, when impossible, 145
*Koan (kung-an*, C), 24 ff., 27, 36, 45 f.
Kwasan (He-shan) (*d.* 960), 76 f.
*Kwats(u) (ho*, C), 27, 45, 158 f.
Kweishan, see I-san
*Kyogai*, see 'environment'
Kyogen (Hsing-yen), 161 f.
Kyozan (Yang-shan) (804-890), 171 f.

*Lankavatara Sutra* quoted, 51
'Leaving no footsteps,' 150 f.
Lin-chi, see Rinzai
'Lions, the six', 189 f.
Literature of Zen, 44—5

MAHAKASYAPA, 12
*Mahaparinirvana Sutra*, doctrine of Buddha-nature in, 195
*Mahapitaka Brahmaraja, Dialogue of Buddha and*, 12, 45
*Mahaprajna*, 99—100
*Maha-prajna-paramita* ('transcendental wisdom'), Hui-neng on, 29 ff.
Man and Nature, 178 ff., 182 f.
*Mano-vijnana* ('intellect', S), 190
Marrow, Bodhidharma's, 23
Ma-tsu, see Baso
*Milinda, Questions of King (Milinda-panha, ca.* 200 B.C.), 14
Mind as ultimate truth in *Lankavatara Sutra*, 51, 54 f.
Mind and Nature, limits of, 54
Mind, eternal, 169
Ming, enlightenment of, 17 f.
'Mirror, the ancient,' 111, 160; see also *Bodhi*-tree
*Mondo* ('question and answer'), 109 ff., 165 ff.
Moon, the second, 191
Mount Vulture, discourse on, 12
'Mountains are mountains,' 187

Myosho, 63, 67 f.
Mysticism, Buddhist and Christian, 21, 74–6, 81 f.

NAGASENA, 14
Name, 192 ff.
Nangaku (Nan-yueh), 18 f.
Nansen (Nan-ch'uan) (d. 834), 140
Naturalism, human and animal, 141
Nature, Western ideas of, 176 f., 179 f.
Nature and Zen, 176 ff., 189 ff., 197 ff., 204
No-mind, moment of, 190; see also cit-taksana
'No paintings can do justice to it,' (Goso), 71
Northern School of Zen, 15
Northrop, on 'undifferentiated continuum', 119
'Nose', 186 ff.

OBAKU (Huang-po) (d. 850), 25 ff., 44 ff., 68 ff.
Objective view of Nature, 182 f.
'One Word,' 149 f., 161 f., 171
Oriental mind as opposed to Western, 40 f.
'Original eternal reason,' Ganto on, 76
'Originally Pure,' 165, 167, 192 f.
Otto, R., 79

PANTHEISM, 21, 94
Paramita ('transcendence,' S), 55; see also Mahaprajnaparamita
Patriarch, 6th, see Hui-neng
Patriarchal system, end of, 19
Patriarchs, 28 Indian, of Zen, 13
Persecutions of Buddhism in China, 34, 131 f.
Plain language in Zen, 131, 133, 150, 158 f.
'Pointing directly to one's Mind', 54 f.
Post, 195–6
Prajna, 55, 85–128, 137 f., 144–6; Hui-neng on, 31–3
Prajnacara, 31 f.
Prajnadharma, 32
Prajna-intuition, 88 ff., 147, 159 f.
Prajnaparamita, 55; Hui-neng on, 29 ff; Sucandra on (in Gandavyuha Sutra), 49 ff.
Prajnatara, 27th Indian Patriarch, Bodhidharma's teacher, 13
'Primary face', 184 ff.
'Primary Man,' 102 ff., 119
Pu shih, 151 f.
Pu shuo po ('do not tell outwardly,' C), 133, 159 f.
'Pure subjectivity', 187 f., 203 f.

QUIETIST tendencies ended by Hui-neng, 16

RATIONALISM and Zen, 130 f., 136 f., 201
Reality (svabhava, S), 54 f.
Reality and symbols, 23
'Revolving' the sutra, 114, 127
Rinzai (Lin-chi) (d. 867), 16, 20, 23 f., 25–8, 56, 68–70, 132, 159, 163
Ryuge and Tokusho, 97

Saddharma-pundarika Sutra, 175
Salvation, 202

Samadhi ('absorption'), 38 f., 127
Samapatti ('equilibrium'), 38 f.
Samatha ('tranquillity'), 38 f.
Samurai, 7, 35
Satori ('understanding,' J), 166, 194
Schools of Zen, 15 f.
'Seal of the Spirit,' 13, 15
Seccho (Hsueh-tou), compiler of Hekigan-shu, 205
'Second moon,' 191
Seigen (Ch'ing-yuen) (d. 740), 18 f.
Sekiso (Shih-shuang) (807–888), 52 f., 194
Sekito (Shih-t'ou) (700–790), 58 f., 109 f,. 142 f., 148, 159
Self, i.e. Reality, 109 ff., 112
Self-destruction, fallacious views on, 52
Self-Essence, Hui-neng on, 30 f.
Self-hypnotism not dhyana, 42 ff.
Self-realization, Sucandra on (Ganda-vyuha Sutra), 50 f.
Seng-ts'an (d. 606), 15.
Seppo (Hsueh-feng) (822–908), 200
Shao-lin monastery, 14
Shen-hsiu, see Jinshu
Shen-hui (Jinne), 138 f., 144
Shen Kuang (afterwards Hui-k'o C, Yeka J), 2nd Chinese Patriarch, 15
Shih-mo (C), see Suchness
Shinro (Chen-lang), 58
Shobi (Ch'u-wei), 171 ff.
Sitting idly, Yakusan on, 58 f., 142
'Six lions,' 189 f.
Six senses, 189 f.
Skin, Bodhidharma's, 23
Soji (Tsung-ch'ih), nun, 23
Sokei source, 97, 126 f.
Sono mama (J), see Suchness
Soto (Ts'ao-tung), 16, 20
Southern School of Zen, 15 f.
Soyen Shaku, Rev., 38 ff.
Sozan (Ts'ao-shan), 62 f.
Special transmission outside the scriptures, 48 f.
"Speak! Speak!," Rinzai and the novice, 56
Spinoza's scientia intuitiva and prajna, 47 f.
Staff, uses of, 86 ff., 125 f., 196
Subjectivity in Zen, 183, 188 ff.
Sucandra (Gandavyuha Sutra), 49 ff.
Succession in Zen, importance of, 45
Suchness (tathata, S), 72, 74, 121, 188, 204; defined, 141 n.
Sudden enlightenment, Dr. Hu Shih's view of, 131; reply to, 137 ff.
Sudhana (Gandavyuha Sutra), 49 ff.
Sunyata ('Emptiness', S), 30, 80; (=prajna), 101, 115, 117, 119, 141 n., 145, 188, 204
Svabhava, see Reality

T'ANG dynasty (618-907), importance of for Zen, 19 f., 127
Tanka (Tan-hsia) (738-824), 127 f.
Tao, 112
'Tao is everyday thought,' Baso (Ma-tsu) on, 139 f.
Tao-hsin, see Doshin
Taoism and Zen, 33 f.
Tao-sheng, see Dosho
Tao-yo, see Doiku

Tea, cup of, 173, 174 f.
Tendai (T'ien-t'ai) School, 163
'Three pounds of flax,' 27, 46, 134
Time and timelessness, 153 f., 188
To of Kokutai, 111
Tokuichi of Ryugeji, 110
Tokusan (Te-shan) (779–865), 54, 126,
    159, 184
Tokusho (Teh-shao) (890–971), 96–100
'Tomorrow,' Zembi on, 116 f.
Tongo Yomon Ron (J, Essentials of Sud-
    den Enlightenment by Daishu Yekai),
    44 f.
Tozan (Tung-shan) (806–869), 27, 167
    f.
Tradition, Zen attitude to, 11 f.
Trance not dhyana, 42 ff.
Transcendental Wisdom, see Prajnapara-
    mita
Transcendental "yes," 141
Transmission, special, outside of Scrip-
    tures, 48 f.
Transmission of the Lamp, Records of
    the (Zen history by Taoyuan, A.D.
    1004), 22 ff., 44, 52 ff., 58 ff., 82 f.,
    148 ff., 150 ff., 165 ff., 198 ff., 201 f.
Transmission of the Mind, On the, by
    Obaku (Huang-po), 45
Trap, caught in own (Goso), 71, 73
Truth, stage of, Kwasan on, 76
Ts'ao-tung, see Soto
Tsung-ch'ih, see Soji
Tsung-mi (Shu-mitsu) on Shenhui,
    139 f., 144
Tung-huang MSS., 9, 45
Tun-wu Yao-men Lu (C, Essentials of
    Sudden Enlightenment by Taichu
    Hui-hai), 44 f.
UMMON (Yun-men) (d. 949), 88, 125 f.,
    134
'Undifferentiated continuum' (North-
    rop), 119
Ungan Donjo (Yun-yen T'an-sheng)
    (d. 841), 152, 189 ff.
Unknown knowledge, 146 f., 162

'Unthinkable,' see acintya
Utpala (lotus), 12

VAIROCANA-BUDDHA, 192 f.
'Vast emptiness,' Bodhidharma on, 14;
    see also sunyata
Vijnana ('reason,' S), 85 ff., 124, 145 f.
Vipasyana ('contemplation', S), 163
Vulture, Mt., 12

'WALL-GAZING brahmin' (Bodhidharma),
    14
Water, crying for, 200
Watts, Alan, 8
Wei Lang, see Hui-neng
Wen-ta, see mondo
Wen-yen, see Ummon
Will and intuition in prajna, 55
Wistaria, comparison with, 62 f., 71, 73
Word, one, 149 f., 161 f., 171
Work, Chinese and Indian views of,
    155 f.
Wu, Emperor, 13 f.

YAKUSAN Igen (Yao-shan Wei-yen) (754–
    834), 58 f., 142 f., 149 ff., 189
Yejaku (name dissected), 171 f.
Yeka (Hui-k'o), disciple of Bodhid-
    harma, 23; see also Shen Kuang
Yengo (Yuan-wu), 71, 73
Yeno, see Hui-neng
Yentoku of Yentsu-in, 110
Yesai, introduced Rinzai Zen to Japan
    (1191), 20
Yikwan, 91
Yo of Kori, 110
Yun-men, see Ummon

Zazen, 37
Zen, basic features of, 11 f.
Zen beyond understanding, 159 f.
Zen-experience, 61 ff., 71 ff., 82 ff.
Zen, meaning of, as opposed to dhyana,
    162
Zenna (J), 12